Yanantin and Masintin in the Andean World

YANANTIN AND MASINTIN IN THE ANDEAN WORLD

COMPLEMENTARY DUALISM IN MODERN PERU

Hillary S. Webb

University of New Mexico Press
ALBUQUERQUE

First paperbound printing, 2012
Paperbound ISBN: 978-0-8263-5073-2

18 17 16 15 14 13 12   1 2 3 4 5 6 7

LIBRARY OF CONGRESS CATALOGING-IN-PUBLICATION DATA

Webb, Hillary S., 1971–
Yanantin and masintin in the Andean world : complementary dualism in modern
Peru / Hillary S. Webb.
p. cm.
Includes bibliographical references and index.
ISBN 978-0-8263-5072-5 (cloth : alk. paper) — ISBN 978-0-8263-5074-9 (electronic)
1. Quechua philosophy. 2. Quechua cosmology.
3. Quechua Indians—Rites and ceremonies. 4. Shamanism—Peru.
5. Dualism. 6. Mind and body. 7. Space and time. I. Title.
F2230.2.K4W43 2012
985´.00498323—dc23
2011019069

DESIGN AND LAYOUT: MELISSA TANDYSH
Composed in 10.5/14 Minion Pro
Display type is Italian Old Style MT Std

To all those who walk with their tails straight up.

And

(of course)

to Carl

CONTENTS

ILLUSTRATIONS

ACKNOWLEDGMENTS

WHEN WE ARE KIDS, our parents teach us to say "thank you" when someone does something nice for us. Over time, in many circumstances, this social ritual becomes simply an automatic response. But then there are moments in our lives when we step back and take inventory of where we are, where we have come from, and who has helped us to get there. In doing so, there is (at least I find) a somewhat overwhelming realization of how many people influence the course of our lives and, as a result, how tied into each other's destinies we all are. What I find particularly eerie is the thought of how different our lives might have been if we were to remove any one element—one person, one circumstance, one moment of chance or fate—that influenced us in even the smallest of ways. Where might we be had we not made that phone call, had we not kept that lunch meeting, had we *kept* that lunch meeting? It is at times like these, when we take the time to really consider the individuals who have influenced the course of our lives, that the words "thank you" take on their fullest meaning and, yet, at the same time, hardly seem to suffice.

It is with that sense of eerie, overwhelming gratitude that I find myself calling to mind all the people whose presence and influence were integral to the researching, writing, and publishing of this book.

I am extremely grateful to have attended Saybrook University, an institution that expects the highest levels of academic rigor from its students while at the same time encouraging experimentation and innovation within one's research methods and subject matter. It was there that I found a group of mentors who were willing to follow me on this journey. In particular, I would like to thank Dr. Steven Pritzker for heading my dissertation committee and for his encouragement, support, and creative intelligence. Deepest thanks also go to the rest of my committee, Dr. Stanley Krippner and Dr. Jurgen Kremer, for pushing me past my own blind spots and limitations so that I could delve ever deeper into this material. A very special thank-you goes to my Saybrook advisor, Dr. Stephen Khamsi, for his guidance, support, and exceptional listening and reflecting abilities. Special love and gratitude go to my Saybrook friends and colleagues who made the whole journey not only intellectually stimulating, but more fun than I ever expected it to be: Alisa Huntington, Angel Morgan, and Sarah Kass.

And, of course, my Andean research participants. How do you thank an entire culture for envisioning a stunningly intricate and elegant philosophical model, one that I believe holds great beauty and promise for anyone looking for an alternative to the antagonistic vision of existence that the Western world oftentimes creates? My hope, my intent, is that this research project as a whole has been one long act of gratitude to the Andean people who have developed, and continue to uphold, this complementary vision of the world. I would like to thank those who acted as representatives of this cultural model—my research participants. In particular, I would like to acknowledge my two primary participants, Amado and Juan Luis. Although "thank you" can never fully express the gratitude that I feel for all the treasures they have given me through their words, by way of their example, and by pushing me to have my own experience of this complementary worldview, here I will say, *muchisimas gracias, hermanitos. Por todo.* Special thanks go to the friends and colleagues who helped my fieldwork unfold: Bonnie Glass-Coffin, Kevin Santillo, Holly Wissler, and Flynn Donovan. Big thanks go to the University of New Mexico Press selection committee and to the UNM Press editorial and production staff for their hard work putting this book together. Thanks also go to my agent, Stephany Evans, for her advice and support.

Then there are those individuals who, while perhaps not directly involved in the creation of this research project, were nonetheless essential to this process. Thank you to my mother and stepfather and my sister and brother-in-law for always being a source of support, guidance, and enthusiasm. To Ben and Rebecca, my nephew and niece, thank you for being two of the most genuine and kind people I have ever met. You both inspire me to do this work, to search for ways of creating a more peaceful and complementary world for all its future inhabitants. Thank you also goes to dear friends who supported me along the way: Leslie Adams, Ken Blonder, Patricia Boissevain, Bonnie Bufkin, the Cooley Boys, Patricia Fontaine, Ayana Gordon, Adam Jennison, Tom Lepore, Will MacDonald, Karen Malik, Michael Mannion and Trish Corbett, Liza Munroe, Maddi Wallach, and Beth Wellwood.

Finally, I began these acknowledgments reflecting on how certain people influence the course of events in such direct and positive ways that it is somewhat frightening to consider where our lives would be had we not, say, run into them one afternoon 12 years ago at Ceres Bakery. If there is anyone whose presence has most influenced this project—most influenced my life, perhaps—it is Carl Hyatt, whose beautiful photos appear throughout the book. For you, *Carlitos lindo*, I reserve the greatest thanks. I'd be somewhere without you, but it sure wouldn't be here.

FIGURE 2: © Carl A. Hyatt, 2003, *Despacho*

INTRODUCTION

The Complement of Difference

THE FIRST TIME I heard the term *yanantin* was back in 2000, when I accompanied a group of people to Peru to learn about the indigenous spiritual philosophies as they exist in that region of the world.[1] It was May 21, and we were sitting in the Sacred Valley, watching the *kuraq akulleq*[2] don Manuel Q'espi construct a *despacho*—a ceremonial offering to the spirits of the earth. On a large white piece of paper, don Manuel created a kind of mandala from a variety of symbolic objects—coca leaves, flowers, confetti, llama fetus and llama fat, tiny figurines in the shape of ladders, caballeros, skirted women, trees, stars, and so on. Each object carried a specific intent for the health of individual, community, and planet.

One of the first items to be included, placed right in the center of the *despacho*, was a small figurine in the form of a human being. The figure was split down the middle, with one half of it colored yellow, the other half pink.

"This is *yanantin*," don Manuel told us as he placed it on the paper. "Complementary opposites."

As I would later discover, one of the most well-known and defining characteristics of indigenous Andean[3] thought is its adherence to a philosophical model[4] based in what is often referred to as a "dualism[5] of complementary terms" (Ajaya, 1983, p. 15) or, simply, a "complementary dualism" (Barnard & Spencer, 2002, p. 598). Similar to Chinese Taoism, Andean philosophy views the opposites of existence (such as male/female, dark/light, inner/outer) as *inter*dependent and essential parts of a harmonious whole. Because existence is believed to be dependent upon the tension and balanced interchange between the polarities, there is a very definite ideological *and* practical commitment within indigenous Andean life to bringing the seemingly conflicting opposites into harmony with one another without destroying or altering either one.[6]

Although I did not know all this at the time, the phrase *complementary opposites* struck me immediately. There was something poetic about it, something that gave me chills when I heard it. Perhaps it caught my attention because it illustrated a perspective that seemed to be in such stark contrast to most "Western"[7] philosophical models, which have historically tended toward a "dualism of antithetical terms" (Ajaya, 1983, p. 15)—the view that the opposites are incompatible and are therefore engaged in an eternal antagonism and struggle for dominance. This antagonistic split shows up in much of Western thought, such as the religious dichotomies of sacred versus profane, spirit versus flesh, Absolute Good versus Absolute Evil, and so on. It plays a major role in our philosophical constructs, the most obvious of these being the debates over the primacy of mind/consciousness versus that of the physical body. As a result, much of Western thought within both spiritual and secular domains has been an attempt to prove once and for all which half of any given polarity is more constant and unchanging, and, therefore, which is more real or primary. Less accepted is the potential for their interdependence.

Psychologically speaking, this devotion to what Carl Jung (1953/1956) referred to as "neurotic one-sidedness" (p. 42) presents itself in a certain intolerance of the complexity of the psyche, one that often results in a compulsion to eliminate all paradoxes and seeming contradictions of the human condition.

A 2007 *Time* article titled "What Makes Us Moral" gives an example of this. The article begins with the following sentiment:

> If the entire human species were a single individual, that person would long ago have been declared mad. The insanity would not lie

in the anger and darkness of the human mind—though it can be a black and raging place indeed. And certainly it wouldn't lie in the transcendent goodness of that mind—one so sublime, we fold it into a larger "soul." The madness would lie instead in the fact that both of those qualities, the savage and the splendid, can exist in one creature, one person, often in one instant. (Kluger, 2007, p. 54)

According to this statement, it doesn't matter whether we choose the "splendid" or the "savage" as long as we align ourselves thoroughly and completely with that one side without deviation. Only then can we be considered healthy and sane.

It was my dismay over what I considered to be the overwhelming tendency for Western culture to fall into crippling psychological "one-sidedness" along with my corresponding fascination with the Andean complementary perspective that prompted me, six years after that initial trip, to devote my doctoral work to studying the concept of *yanantin* as it is understood by indigenous Andeans living in or near the city of Cuzco, Peru. I chose to focus on the experience of complementary dualism in Peru rather than any other part of the Andean region because of my personal and intellectual familiarity with the country's philosophical beliefs and practices. Of all the Andean regions, Peru has the most scholarly literature written about it, which I felt would ground my study within a lineage of historical, ethnological, and philosophical research. In the beginning of the study, I considered heading into the high Andes to work with the Q'ero, a people considered by some to be the last members of the Inca lineage. Given the remote location in which they live, the Q'ero and many of the other Quechua-speaking groups of that region still maintain a relatively "traditional" lifestyle. This, I reasoned, would give me a chance to understand *yanantin* in its most unadulterated form.

However, during the initial days of my fieldwork, my focus shifted as I found myself pulled into the world of the indigenous Andeans living in or near the city of Cuzco in central Peru and, in particular, the world of the Cusqueño shamans who inhabit this region.[8] In Inca times, Cuzco was considered the "navel of the world" and as such was a meeting place for the diverse groups that made up the Inca Empire. Similarly today, Cuzco is a kind of cultural melting pot, a blend of indigenous Andeans whose lineage goes back to thousands of years before the Spanish Conquest, mixed-blood mestizos, and gringo ex-patriots from just about everywhere around the world. Therefore, neither Peru in general nor Cuzco in particular is a stranger to the influence of foreign ideologies. With the Spanish Conquest in the sixteenth century came the enforcement of a set of radically different religious and political values upon the native population (Andrien, 2001; Silverblatt, 1987; Taussig, 1980). Despite Peru's independence from Spain in 1821, the introduction of Western economic practices continued to cause changes in basic social and economic relations in even the most remote regions of the country (Apffel-Marglin, 1998; Fernandez, 1998; Fernandez & Gutierrez, 1996; Joralemon & Sharon, 1993).[9]

And yet, despite this, many scholars argue that although it may seem that the original Andean complementary model is being replaced by Western conceptions and influences, the Andean allegiance to complementary dualism as the underlying philosophical construct remains intact. Rather than representing a *conversion* to Western ideologies and practices, they suggest, the Andean people tend toward "an adaptation to—not an adoption of—the [Western] ethos" (Joralemon & Sharon, 1993).

Palomino (1971) suggested that

> [t]he Andean man . . . continues to live within the structural model of his remote ancestors, but with a new symbolic and actual reality founded on historical events. It is possible that he may be on the brink of a radical change in his main characteristics, but his dualism goes on even under new conditions. (p. 86)

Rather than out-and-out conversion, it seems that something more like a syncretism takes place in the Andean world whenever some new idea is thrown into the philosophical mix. This was certainly reflected among my research participants. For example, despite their deep devotion to continuing the traditional spiritual lineage of their ancestors, several chose to be married in the Catholic church in addition to observing the original, earth-honoring marriage ceremonies. Similarly, many of the healers and shamans with whom I worked have statues of Catholic saints on their altars, which sit alongside representations of llamas and condors and other traditional symbols. Likewise, during the opening of a spiritual ceremony, one of my participants invoked "Master Jesus" in addition to Pachacamac, Wiracochan, and an assortment of other ancient Andean divinities.

More recently, a new influence has emerged on the Andean spiritual scene in the form of the "New Age." It is noteworthy that the New Age movement, having borrowed many of its beliefs, symbols, and practices from indigenous cultures, and then combined them with other teachings from around the world, has brought these beliefs back to Cuzco in a new, regurgitated, and reimagined form. A stroll down the tourist section of the city shows that Cuzco is adapting to even this new influence, taking it in, and drawing on it for its own purposes.[10] Listening to my research participants, it quickly became evident that the language and ideas of the New Age movement have influenced the ways in which many of them talk about the concept of *yanantin*. Words like *chakra* and *karma* have become part of lexicon and a means by which they explain certain concepts. While some may consider this a tragic dilution of a once "pure" ideology, I believe that the inclusiveness of the Andean ideology and its willingness to "use what works" (whether part of a several-thousand-year-old lineage or something they have picked up from watching *The Matrix*) is one of the hallmarks and great strengths of an ideology that does not make sharp either/or, good/bad distinctions. It is, I believe, also what has allowed this ideology to not only endure, but also to thrive and evolve on its own terms. While, as a researcher, the addition of these foreign elements added to the complexity and sometimes seemingly contradictory nature[11] of Andean complementary dualism as it exists today, at the same time, this syncretism allowed me to see certain dimensions of Andean complementary dualism that I might not have otherwise.

Having settled on a specific region and set of participants to work with, my intent was to conduct a traditional ethnographic study in which I would focus on recording the experience of *yanantin* as seen through the eyes of indigenous Cusqueños and, in particular, Cusqueño shamans. While acknowledging that true objectivity is impossible, traditional ethnographies are intended to describe the lived experience of a particular culture-sharing group. Data is collected through interviewing one's research participants, observing them in their daily lives, and on occasion participating in their secular and spiritual activities in order to achieve an emic or "insider's" perspective. With this methodology as my basis of understanding, my intent was to shed light on the question "What is the psycho-spiritual experience of *yanantin* for indigenous Andeans living in the city of Cuzco, Peru?"

However, as will be illustrated in the first few chapters of this book, immediately upon arriving in Cuzco for my first fieldwork trip, it became apparent that my research participants were not going to let me get away with objectifying this complex philosophical ideal in this way. In order to understand *yanantin*, they told me over and over and over again, I would have to *experience* it. Although I initially felt an overwhelming sense of intellectual frustration and dismay at the seeming lack of "facts" that I was receiving as a result, over time I came to understand the wisdom of this approach—that attempting to create a kind of objective study by relying solely on observation and interviewing was neither possible nor desirable when attempting to understand the experience of Andean complementary dualism. In fact, it seemed to me that doing so conflicted with the very epistemological principles of the subject matter that I was trying to understand and illuminate. That is, that "truth" lies in the *complementary* nature of the relationship between subject and object, not in their division.

As Fernandez (1998) wrote when describing the essence of the Andean indigenous worldview,

> [h]ere nothing remains static. This is why a theory of the world or a methodology does not belong here. Here the only thing that belongs is an open and continuous conversation, with the active participation of all those of us who are the Andean world. . . . [H]ere there is no room for fundamentalism or essentialism. We are the world of love and nurturance, of exuberance, of voluptuousness, of exultation. There is here no manner of substratum that would sustain any intellectualism or dogmatism. This is no context for moralism or Puritanism. Here the one truth cannot live. (p. 141)

As Fernandez wrote, and as my research participants would concur, according to the indigenous Andean worldview in its most idealized form, existence is a collection of constantly changing circumstances. Relationships between one thing and another are always in flux, and so it is generally acknowledged that one explanation, one "Truth," cannot capture the levels of complexity unfolding within the world from moment to moment. To choose one theory over another is to deny an essential part of existence and completely miss the point of the Andean vision of the complementary nature of the world.

As I will attempt to show throughout this book, making this shift from being an "objective" social scientist to finally achieving a trust in my own first-person experience only occurred after undergoing several radical shifts in consciousness that convinced me that I could acquire knowledge in this way.[12] As this epistemological shift occurred, my relationship to my research topic transformed as well. While in the beginning my motivation for undertaking this project centered around my perception of and concern about a generalized malaise within the Western psyche as a whole, I came to realize that I must acknowledge my *own* antagonistic relationship to existence—the battle between the "splendor" and "savagery" taking place within my own psyche on both conscious and unconscious levels, which affected the way I related to myself, to others, and to the world around me. I came to realize that the study I wanted to do required that I not only attain an intellectual understanding of how my participants relate to *yanantin* as a philosophical ideal, but that I use myself as a "subject" in this study by attempting to make a shift in my own consciousness from that of Western antagonism to one of "complementarity."

And so, by the end of my first fieldwork trip, the question driving my research project changed from the more objectively focused question of "What is the psychological experience of *yanantin* for the indigenous Andeans living in the city of Cuzco, Peru?" to the more personally driven "What is the experience of a Western researcher attempting to understand and integrate Andean complementary dualism, and what does it reveal about the essence of the phenomenon?" Because of this shift in focus, I realized I needed a new research methodology, one that would allow me to gain insight into the psychological experience of Andean complementary dualism from a *subjective* point of view.[13] Because of this I eventually decided to conduct my study as an "autoethnography."

As the latter half of the word implies, auto*ethnography* is similar to a traditional ethnography in that its aim is to describe and interpret the behaviors and customs of a culture-sharing group (Creswell, 1998). While within a traditional ethnography the inner experience of the researcher is alluded to but not focused on, in an *autoethnography*, the researcher's first-person experience of the culture and/or phenomenon is not only the primary focus but also the *means by which* data are collected, analyzed, and interpreted. While the term "autoethnography" is at times used to refer to research relating to an ethnographer's own ethnic or cultural group (also called "native ethnography" [Chang, 2008, p. 44]), it is also applied to ethnographic narratives such as this in which a researcher's personal experiences of and reactions to being a cultural outsider provide context for the cultural analysis and interpretation.

Ellis (2004) described autoethnography as writing that connects the personal to the cultural, social, and political aspects of a phenomenon. Chang (2008) explained it as a methodology that "utilizes the researchers' autobiographical data to analyze and interpret their cultural assumptions" (p. 9). In order to do so, the researcher must make continual comparisons between the "objective" characteristics of the phenomenon as lived by the cultural participants and the researcher's own "bodily, cognitive, emotional, and spiritual experience" (Ellis, 2004, p. 30). What results from this inner-outer dialectic is a narrative account of the researcher's first-person experience that is both artistically and academically engaging (Chang, 2008).

Despite my belief that autoethnography was the ideal methodology for conducting this particular study, the decision to eschew conventional wisdom that the researcher and the researched be kept separate(ish) brought with it a number of epistemological and professional concerns. Because autoethnography requires a more personal and literary approach, I found that I had some anxiety about how such an unorthodox methodology would be received, both by my dissertation committee and by my peers in the field. In certain circles, autoethnography is considered to be the ultimate in researcher self-indulgence, oftentimes confessional to the point of providing insight only into the mind of the researcher rather than the phenomenon itself (Chang, 2008; Ellis, 2004). Because of this, I realized that if I were to complete the project with any success and credibility, I would have to find innovative ways of using my subjective experience as a means by which I could collect, analyze, and interpret data that would illuminate the lived experience of Andean complementary dualism.

While the primary methodology is that of an autoethnography, my study became a triangulation of data-gathering methods that included both the more traditional and objective methodological approaches such as literature review, interview, observation, and participant observation and also the subjective reflections of my own experience. My belief was that, when brought together, these methods would create a multidimensional, multivoiced interpretation of Andean complementary dualism. For example, by conducting an in-depth review of the existing literature throughout the research process, I was able to obtain a sense of the history of Andean complementary dualism, as well as how complementary dualism has been and is currently understood by scholars and other writers. In order to collect original data about the topic, over the course of my fieldwork I conducted a series of interviews with eight Andean participants. Of the eight participants I worked with, four of them are considered "shamans," as they have been extensively trained in the traditional spiritual philosophies and practices of the region. As the healers, philosophers, and spiritual guides of their communities, their profession requires that they have an intimate understanding of *yanantin* in its sacred and secular forms. Therefore, these seemed to be the ideal individuals with whom to work. The remaining four participants were individuals who had either a scholarly or personal interest in *yanantin*. All participants were chosen based on having demonstrated an ability to think both reflectively and critically about their experiences of the phenomenon of *yanantin*, with the shamans speaking more experientially, and the others regarding it in a way that was more broad and observational. Although some of my participants had a smaller role than others (some appear only once within the narrative, while the voice of others recurs over several sections) each provided an essential insight in my own understanding of the role of complementary dualism within their lives and in the lives of others.

In addition to these interviews, the more traditionally "ethnographic" aspect of my research included observing my participants in spiritual and secular settings. My aim was to take note of anything that my participants did or said that conveyed a sense of the phenomenon of *yanantin*. During this time, I also observed the interactions of anonymous individuals who I encountered in the streets, in the markets, and anywhere else I happened to be. While observation is hardly an accurate means of understanding such an internal and subjective issue as psychological experience, what my observations did do was prompt me to ask certain questions that I might not have otherwise considered. This method of "observation" also included "participant observation," with me joining my research participants in many of their spiritual and secular activities. Ethnographically speaking, the act of participant observation straddles the line of objective and subjective research, and for me this was a first step in marrying the various subjective and objective perspectives together into a multidimensional whole.

All these methods are fairly standard practice in conducting an ethnographic exploration. However, the method I had chosen—autoethnography—required that I go even deeper into my personal experience. In order to do so, I needed to mine my psyche, to use my inner experience as the method by which I could illuminate what it is to see the world through the lens of complementary dualism. The most effective means I found of doing this was through a daily ritual of "rapid-fire memoing." Every evening, I would compile the notes that I had made throughout the day while they were still fresh in my mind. At this point, I wrote down any additional thoughts that came to me about the phenomenon, including any insights I had had, the conclusions I had reached, and the ideas I had for further points to be elucidated. Once I had completed that process, I then engaged in stream-of-consciousness journaling in which I wrote down, without censorship, any thoughts about my personal relationship to the phenomenon. During this process, I took special care to note occasions when I had a strong emotional response to something that my participants had told me, whether that was disbelief, anger, joy, awe, or any other noticeable reaction. In the early stages of my research, I discovered that these stream-of-consciousness journal entries were an important way to uncover the unconscious structures within the philosophical model of my own culture as well that of my participants. The process of observing and taking note of my emotional reactions thus became an important form of data-gathering in and of itself that I eventually used to identify cross-cultural dissonances that occurred between my Western worldview and the one in which I was engaging. Anything that elicited a strong emotional response within me served as a tap on the shoulder that I had come across data about Andean complementary dualism that had challenged the unconscious cultural assumptions in which I was raised. By paying attention to these emotional "jolts," my subjective, emotional experience revealed essential components of understanding the Andean worldview.

After gathering data by way of scholarly research, interviewing, observation, participant observation, and journal writing, I moved into the "analysis" phase of the research. To analyze the data, I decided to use techniques outlined by Ellis (2004) and Chang (2008), both of whom suggested that, in an autoethnography, analysis and interpretation result in a "naturalistic generalization," meaning that the narrative "brings 'felt' news from one world to another and provides opportunities for the reader to have vicarious experience of things told" (Ellis, 2004, p. 195). The analysis should highlight connections between the perspective of the researcher and that of the participants (Chang, 2008; Ellis, 2004). In accordance with data analysis techniques presented by Chang (2008), I began the analysis phase by reviewing the accumulated data, searching for recurring topics, themes, and patterns that appeared to be both personally and culturally relevant to the study of the phenomenon. I then sorted these excerpts into various categories of shared meaning. For example, in a category called *Epistemology*, I placed excerpts of interviews with my participants that highlighted Andean ways of knowing and my personal reaction to these ideas. During the sorting process, I made a conscious effort not to "mix meanings" by comparing my personal interpretations with those of my participants. My intent was to try to keep my participants' statements as isolated entities rather than projecting meaning onto their experience based on my own explanation and experience. After this creation of categories reached a saturation point, I sorted and reread the field notes, journal entries, and interview transcriptions from which I had taken these excerpts in order to further assure myself that the categories that I had placed them in still seemed appropriate.

Once I had attained a certain amount of confidence that I had provided a meaningful and personally accurate structure to the collected data, I then proceeded with the "interpretation" phase of my analysis. The purpose of the interpretation phase was to uncover the essence of my experience engaging in a personal and intellectual dialogue with the phenomenon. I utilized a five-stage process based on the work of Richardson (1994) and later further refined based on Handwerker's (2008) method of identifying and working with emotions during the psychotherapeutic process. These five stages allowed me to arrive at the core of my experience in a way that illuminates the phenomenon and its essence of meaning.

The interpretation technique included the following stages:

1. *Identifying the emotion as it arises.* For the purposes of this study, I considered an "emotion" to be any highly charged psychological response that revealed something about my unconscious nature and how I engage with the world.

2. *Labeling the emotion.* It is often easy to confuse one emotion with another. For example, anger, when explored more deeply, is often fear in disguise. To be as precise as possible when identifying the emotion that is elicited, during this stage of the interpretation phase, I referred to the Feelings Inventory provided by The Center for Nonviolent Communication (2005). This chart provides opportunities to identify the subtleties of emotional experience so that one can be as precise as possible when identifying the emotional content of one's personal story. For example, under the heading of *Exhilarated* are related words such as *blissful* and *enthralled.* Under the heading of *Pain* are words such as *anguished* and *lonely.* Attaining this level of specificity was an essential aspect of the interpretation process, for it revealed complexities of meaning within my own consciousness as well as those of the phenomenon itself.

3. *Emotional motivation.* Next, I asked myself, "What does this feeling want to accomplish?" and/or "In what ways did it bring me closer to discovering deep meanings about the phenomenon?" For example, a sensation of feeling "alienated" or "nervous" signaled that my own psyche was creating resistance to change.

4. *The manifestation of emotion.* Emotional content manifests on many levels at once. During this stage, I explored the ways in which the emotion I had experienced affected my entire being, on both physical and psychological levels. For example, in one instance, the sensation of blood rushing to my face and the feeling of inadequacy arose due to an emotion of "self-consciousness."

5. *Emotion as transformational tool.* The purpose of the analysis phase of my research was to reveal the essence of my psychological experience of Andean complementary dualism. The intent of the fifth and final stage of this process was to determine whether I had integrated this new perspective and, if so, in what ways my psychological life had changed as a result. This was done by way of postfieldwork self-reflection as explicated in the penultimate chapter.

In an autoethnography, the act of writing is considered the primary means of interpreting and illuminating a phenomenon. After completing the interpretation phase, I returned to the categories that I had created and constructed several narratives in which I attempted to create a back-and-forth dialogue between the meanings behind my subjective experience and the meanings described by my participants. In doing so, I attempted to retain the emotional and existential qualities of the experience as they occurred at the time with the hope of creating opportunities for the essence of the phenomenon to come to light. This process resulted in the narrative that comprises this book.

The final stage of my research process was that of validation. Validating the "accuracy" of one's interpretation is particularly difficult in an autoethnography, for within this context the researcher is not trying to make pronouncements about a culture as a whole (although certain ethnographic "facts" do play an important role). Rather, the intent is to convey subjective meanings based on the researcher's personal reflections. What is sought is an overall picture and theory that represents the essence or essences of the researcher's first-person experience with a phenomenon. Regarding my own study, I felt it was important that I address two questions about the validity of the piece. These two questions were (1) "Does the study illuminate certain aspects of Andean complementary dualism in a way that is true to the cultural participants' experience of it?" and (2) "Does the narrative direct an outside reader's attention to those aspects of Western culture that we normally take for granted or are unaware of, thereby providing increasing knowledge of the human condition?"

As researcher, my hope was that by coming as close to the emotional truth of the events that occurred during fieldwork—both my own "truth" and that of my participants—the resulting narrative would achieve significance and meaning on both counts. To determine if I had indeed captured the essence of the phenomenon as lived by my cultural participants, during my final fieldwork trip to Peru I read the resulting narrative to Amado, my primary participant, asking him to comment on whether I had articulated this idea of *yanantin* with full cultural meaning according to his understanding of it. Reading the results of my research to Amado turned out to be both an essential validation process and an additional data-gathering technique. Not only was he able to correct and/or clarify the areas in which my understanding of *yanantin* (and also the understandings of *yanantin* described in the published literature) was unclear or did not reflect his experience, but during this time Amado also added further insight, resulting in a more complete overview of Andean complementary dualism.

Besides attempting to express the meaning that this phenomenon had in the lives of my Andean participants, it felt equally necessary for me to validate that the narrative I had written was effective in its transmission of the data to other Westerners who read it. In an autoethnography, the validity of the research report is in large part determined by the final narrative's rhetorical power—that is, whether it causes the reader to become "emotionally aroused" and "cognitively engaged" (Ellis, 2004, p. 254), thus prompting the reader to reflect more deeply on the phenomenon being examined and its relationship to the reader's own lived experiences. Ellis (2004) proposed that the validity of an autoethnographic study can be determined by asking the question "Does the story have 'naturalistic generalization'?" Or, rather, does the story transmit "'felt' news from one world to another and provide opportunities for the readers to have a vicarious experience of the things told"? (p. 195). Behar (1996) likewise maintained that this kind of self-reflective storytelling "has to take us somewhere we couldn't otherwise get to" (p. 14). The final stage of compiling my report therefore involved having it read by several Western colleagues who then judged the extent of resonance or insight it provided into the phenomenon, including whether this could potentially add valuable intellectual and emotional insight to the lives of others. Portions of their responses and feedback are included in the final chapter of this book in which I further reflect upon the relevance of this particular study and the methodology through which it was created.

In the pages that follow, I have attempted to create a document that pays respect to both the subjective and objective elements that arose as a result of my involvement with Andean complementary dualism. As a partly autobiographical document, this book recounts the personally meaningful experiences that I had while working with my cultural participants, showing by way of personal narrative how diving deeply into the Andean perspective of complementary dualism forced me to come face to face with the limitations and assumptions of my culture of origin's primary paradigm and, on a more personal level, how my culture's philosophical model and its relationship to the opposites had affected me on both conscious and unconscious levels. As I was to discover, "complementary dualism" as a philosophical model provides an understanding of the world so different from that of the Western philosophical model that attempting to understand and integrate Andean philosophies and practices within my own life involved a radical deconstruction in which my habitual ways of viewing the world and self had to be eschewed for oftentimes seemingly contradictory ones. The degree and depth to which my culture's worldview had marked me was something that I had not fully appreciated until I arrived in Peru to begin this work. While this process was frustrating and even distressing at times, as I attempted to understand and integrate indigenous Andean philosophical models and practices, I became more and more conscious of the deep-seated assumptions inherent in my own cultural mind-set. The resulting narrative was intended to make this evident by highlighting certain moments in which a collision of cultural models took place. Each chapter explores a different polarity, illuminating the distinction between Western and Andean ways of conceptualizing these dichotomies through a look at the dialectic that occurs when these two worldviews encounter one another within a singular consciousness. While this is obviously a limited exploration given that it was done using a sample size of one—me—it culminates with a consideration of how my own experience might serve as a psychological stand-in for Westerners in general.

I have also made it part of the scope of this book to include more "objective" historical and cultural "facts" pertaining to the indigenous Andean perspective. That is, in addition to recounting my own personal story, I have included an explanation of certain elements of indigenous Andean social and spiritual life as they are understood by me and by others in the field of Andean studies. These elements come from interviews that I did with my participants during the time of my research and also from facts and figures gained from a review of the literature pertaining to Andean studies. My intent was to ground my own personal story within a well-documented historical and cultural framework, thereby not limiting it to my singular personal opinion, understanding, and experience, but rather providing a multivoiced, multidimensional explication of both the intellectual and the experiential dimensions of the subject matter. This, I hope, makes the book accessible to both academics who wish to gain some scholarly insight into the Andean worldview and general readers who enjoy a story of adventure and psychological exploration. Observant readers will note that the books cited within the narrative are a mix of both scholarly and "popular" literature. The former category includes peer-reviewed ethnographies, theoretical essays, and meta-analyses of Andean cosmology. The latter category, the "popular" (or, some might call it, "New Age") literature, encompasses works that are geared toward readers with a more personal and/or experiential interest in Andean philosophy and practices. Some may take issue with the mixing of these genres, arguing that the two categories are incompatible in a scholarly study such as this. While I agree that it is important to point out that the various texts cited in this book fall into different—some might even call them *opposing*—genres, I do so somewhat begrudgingly and with a certain amount of trepidation that splitting the two into discrete categories does a disservice to them both. First, I don't believe the distinction between the two genres either is or should always be an easy one to make. Second, doing so runs the risk of implying that I believe one to be superior to the other. I do not.

I am, however, realistic that others on both sides of the issue do make such distinctions. Many in the academy tend to exclude and sometimes even vilify the "popular" or "New Age" sources, considering them to lack methodological rigor and scholarly sanctioning. Likewise, there are readers who prefer a more experiential or "user-friendly" understanding of Andean philosophy and who discount the scholarly sources, considering them to be cold and far-removed from the truth of what it is to be a living, breathing human being engaging with these cultural phenomena.

My intent here is not to make the case that one perspective is superior to the other. Far from it. I maintain that both have their strengths and limitations and that those of us interested in the field of Andean studies would be well served to keep an open mind about what each genre has to offer. Therefore, rather than keeping them separate in the in-text citations as some have suggested, I have decided to let the various sources commingle, making the caveat here that while authors of both genres are listed together within a citation, that does not necessarily mean that they all have commensurate opinions on or similar methodological strategies pertaining to any given aspect of Andean complementary dualism. My intent has been to use a variety of sources as a means of highlighting places within both genres of literature that seemed to reflect and echo the perspectives of my research participants. Readers who have a particular preference for one genre or the other can look through the reference section at the end and distinguish with reasonable ease which reference belongs to which category.

Conducting this research study was a remarkable experience for me, teaching me much about the variety of ways in which cultures can make meaning of the world around them, and how deeply attached we become to our own culturally imposed meaning-making strategies. As I hope will be made evident over the course of the narrative that follows, my engagement with Andean complementary dualism had a profound effect on me, in both dramatic and subtle ways, and on both personal and scholarly levels.

FIGURE 3: © Carl A. Hyatt, 2005, Cuzco with Full Moon

CHAPTER ONE

The Knower and the Known

I'M NOT SURE WHY I picked a kangaroo, but I figured that as stuffed animals went, this one would be exotic enough to keep Julián entertained—at least for as long as a two-year-old can be entertained anyway. It had been six years since I had last been to Cuzco, and this was the first time I would be meeting Amado's[1] wife and son.

So strange to be back here again. Sitting in the Plaza de Armas waiting for Amado to arrive, I tried to detect any differences from the last time I was there. If there were changes, they were subtle. Most of the tourist restaurants bordering the plaza were still the same—Tunupa, where I had my first taste of alpaca stew; Ayllu Café and its *jugo especial* ("special juice," indeed—orange, papaya, carrots, beer, molasses . . . if you could extract a liquid from it, it was in there); Mama Africa, where the hip, young vagabonds congregated for movies and socializing. There in the middle of the plaza, small children ran up and down the fountain steps chasing each other and then, when tired, went back to begging for *soles* from sympathetic gringos like me. One had a shoe shining kit and offered to shine my shoes, expertly rebutting my statement that one can't shine hiking boots made of suede and rubber with an emphatic *¡Sí, se puede!* The smell was certainly the same—that strangely delicious combination of diesel gasoline from the taxis circling the square and some musky scent that I always associate with the lanolin from the alpaca wool that is used in textiles there. The latter was probably my imagination, for from where I was sitting, I could hardly have been smelling that. Then again, perhaps the low-oxygen air carried scents farther than at sea level. That could be. I noticed that any time I was above 11,000 feet everything took on a heightened quality that seemed to border on visionary. Small things took on greater significance. Perhaps all overseas travel is like that to a certain extent, but I had never experienced anything quite the way it felt being in Cuzco: that fugue state.

I like the definition my computer's dictionary gives for that word.

Fugue: "A disordered state of mind, in which somebody typically wanders from home and experiences a loss of memory relating only to the previous, rejected environment."

That was exactly how it felt. It was as if one entered into a kind of altered state simply by stepping off the plane. I had arrived two days earlier after what ended up being a nearly 24-hour journey from Boston to Cuzco, deliriously tired and barely able to string two thoughts together in Spanish. Two days of sleeping off the jetlag had taken the edge off my grogginess and loosened the knots in my tongue. Yet, whether it was the altitude or the place itself, I still felt on some level that I was walking around in a dream.

Yes. How strange it was to be there.

It was mid-March, the tail end of the rainy season. The city as a singular entity seemed to be taking a few deep breathes before tourist season began full force. Of course, Cuzco—nicknamed the "Gringo Capital of South America" (Box & Frankham, 2006, p. 64)—is never without a generous sprinkling of nonnatives roaming the streets. Because of its fame as the capital of the Inca Empire, its position as a central location close to many of the country's most ancient and most sacred sites, as well as its reputation as a friendly environment for weary travelers to settle themselves down for a good meal and a good night's sleep, Cuzco has historically been a gateway to the rest of the Andean world, a natural stopover point for travelers. Among these foreign faces were a number of Western expatriates who, for one reason or another, had decided to resettle there permanently. Whenever I came across one of these transplants, I would ask what had drawn him or her to Cuzco. Getting a definitive answer was almost never possible. Most of the time, my question was answered with a few obligatory statements about the people, the climate, or the atmosphere in general. Sometimes the question would cause them to look slightly distressed, as if by asking it I had forced them to step outside the environment that they had become so much a part of and look back at it. Perhaps it was silly of me to even ask. Maybe even a little unfair. There are so many things that cannot be answered in logical terms.

Although I had never lived there longer than a month at a time, having visited Cuzco frequently in the past, I came to understand—at least according to my own terms—what made it such an appealing place. It has been suggested that "there are two Perus: one official, modernized and civilized; the other Indian, backward and primitive, albeit resilient" (sentiment attributed to Vargas Llosa, as described by Apffel-Marglin, 1998, p. 7). Descriptors such as *backward* and *primitive* are, of course, not only racist and ethnocentric but also reveal the ignorance and limitations of Western-influenced ways of conceiving of the world. Still, as an outsider, something about the *essence* of this proposed division felt significant, both regarding Peru in general but perhaps even more so for Cuzco in particular. While there are no doubt *many* Cuzcos—a different Cuzco for each person who experiences it—one can understand the rationale behind this vision of its "twoness" (Maybury-Lewis, 1989a, p. 12). And given that "twoness" was the theme of my research project, it seems appropriate enough to consider it in this way, despite the obvious limitations of trying to analyze a culture and its people in such either/or terms.

Undoubtedly, there is a "modern" Cuzco, one that has kept pace with the passing of time and the demands of a changing world. For those of us even slightly high-maintenance Westerners, Cuzco provides enough comforts and conveniences of home that little is missed. As I sat in the plaza, I could see examples of those surface elements that one might equate with modernity: ATMs, cell phone use, museums, luxury hotels, and universities. Strange, though, to try to identify the things that we equate with modernity. Even the term *modern* itself creates a gap between the necessary and the superfluous, that which takes care of basic, but essential, survival needs and that which we have only somewhat recently grown to believe is indispensable to our existence.

Those were just a few of the pieces composing the modern face of Cuzco. The "other" Cuzco was a Cuzco that seemed immune to the forward march of progress. This was a Cuzco that *endured*. Progress has a fascinating appetite for self-destruction—like the serpent eating its own tail—but while progress had come to Cuzco, it had not yet overcome it. Cuzco remained its own, on its own terms, as if somehow it had found a way to resist the tremendous undertow of history that drags so many places into the homogeneity of modernity. Unlike many cities of the world that have succumbed to Western political, economic, and ideological influences to such a degree that they eventually become more or less replicas of one another, Cuzco seemed impenetrable, seemed to defy outer influence, seemed to defy even time itself. Tucked neatly into the southern Andean chain, Cuzco is surrounded by *apus*, the mountain lords of the Andes. Snow-capped and looming, it is as if the spirits of the place are always there, watching. While outside influences are tolerated, even enjoyed—*for now*—one gets the sense that the energies of the land (both human and nonhuman) might at any moment decide to reclaim it as their own.

In fact, quite frequently they do. A few months after I returned home from my first fieldwork trip, local protestors—sparked by nationalistic pride—shut down the Cuzco airport and blocked the rail line to Machu Picchu, demanding the repeal of new laws that would allow Western luxury hotels to be built near archaeological sites and historic zones.

"*¡Cuzco no se vende!*" they shouted. "Cuzco is not for sale!"

As a result of these protests, the Peruvian Congress modified the laws to allow regional and local governments more power in determining private development around sites of cultural significance (CNN online, 2008).

Because of this—because of many things—Cuzco has retained enough mystery and sense of itself as a unique cultural entity that it makes a person feel as if he or she has escaped the world from which he or she has come and entered a place where past and present coexist in a way that feels almost seamless. From my bench, I could see evidence of this in the massive Inca stonework that provides the architectural basis for modern banks and businesses, still acting as both a metaphorical and literal foundation for the city. In 1650 and 1950, two huge earthquakes destroyed many of the colonial buildings, while the Inca stonemasonry stayed steadfast and true (Box & Frankham, 2006).

Not far from where I was sitting, tucked out of the way of the worn tourist pathways, was the *hampi qhatu*, the "medicine market" or "shamans' market"—a row of small shops selling ceremonial items such as *despacho* bundles—brown paper packets containing various ceremonial items including seeds, confetti, a llama fetus, shells, and small metal figurines. These things were arranged on paper and then burned as an offering to Pachamama, a word that closely equates to our notion of Mother Earth but that also encompasses time and space. No, the spirits of the land had not departed, not in the least, and they still needed to be fed in order to retain the delicate balance of life.

Perhaps the juxtaposition of these "two Cuzcos" was part of the surreality of being there. For me, it was a tangible representation of the Andean commitment to finding the harmonious balance between opposing energies—a philosophy for which their culture is well known. Although the South American Andes consists of a number of contrasting regions (dry, coastal desert and high, looming mountains) as well as various distinct culture-sharing groups that inhabit this area, the multiplicity of indigenous Andean groups is identified as being linked by a certain philosophical belief system through which they interpret reality—a belief system that is based upon a philosophical model known as a "dualism of complementary terms" (Ajaya, 1983, p. 15) or what is simply called a "complementary dualism" (Barnard & Spencer, 2002, p. 598). According to this worldview, everything has a counterpart without which it cannot exist. Existence is seen as being dependent upon, not under threat by, the tension and balanced interchange between the polarities. Therefore, it is believed that if one side of two opposing forces is destroyed or denied, the other will suffer to an equal degree, resulting in disharmony and illness. While not denying the tension created by seemingly contradictory forces such as dark/light, male/female, and so on, within Andean philosophy there is an ideological commitment within social and spiritual life to bringing the opposites into harmony without destroying or altering either one (Allen, 2002; Andrien, 2001; Astvaldsson, 2000; Bastien, 1978; Bolin, 2006; Glass-Coffin, 1998; Harrison, 1989; Harvey, 2006; Heckman, 2003; Isbell, 1978; Joralemon & Sharon, 1993; Mannheim, 1991; Murra & Wachtel, 1986; Seibold, 1992; Silverblatt, 1987; Stone-Miller, 2002; Taussig, 1980; Urton, 1981). Bastien (1978) put it this way: "The struggle in the Andes is an attempt to remove the discrepancies between the analogous terms" (p. 94).

In Quechua, one of the native languages of the highland Andes, this idea of complementary opposites is called *yanantin* and is considered, among people living a traditional or non-Westernized lifestyle, a fundamental life principle (Platt, 1986). Etymologically, the prefix *yana-* means "help," while its suffix *-ntin* means "inclusive in nature, with implications of totality, spatial inclusion of one thing in another, or identification of two elements as members of the same category" (Platt, 1986, p. 245). Some scholars (Urton, 1981) break down the word slightly differently, translating *yana-* as "black" in the sense of "dark" or "obscure," and contrast it to "light" (rather than in the sense of "black" as opposed to "white").

Some scholars have translated *yanantin* as "the complement of difference" (Wilcox, 1999, p. 46). However, when I asked Amado about this particular definition, he was quick to emphasize that it is not the differences that are identified within a *yanantin* relationship but rather what the two energies bring together as a parity.

"For us, *yanantin* doesn't focus on the differences between two beings. That is what disconnects them. Instead, we focus on the qualities that brought them together. That is *yanantin*. We don't really see the differences. That's why we see them as not necessarily opposed, but as complementary. One on its own can't hold everything, can't take care of everything. Not only are they great together, but they *need* to be together. There is no other way. When there is another, it represents extra strength for both."

I first met Amado during one of my earlier visits to Peru and later became reacquainted with him during one of his trips to the United States. It would be good to see him again. Almost 10 years younger than me, Amado had a sweetness and youthful exuberance that was refreshing and contagiously calming. He was raised by his grandparents in Chincheros, a small town high in the hills above Cuzco. When Amado was six, he was struck by lightning, which in the Andean shamanic lineage is traditionally how the neophyte shaman is chosen by the spirits to walk the medicine path. His grandfather, a renowned *paqo* (healer), took this as a sign that he should pass on his teachings—all the stories, ceremonies, rituals, and other wisdom of the lineage that he carried—to his grandson. The early days of Amado's training were done in secret, for even in his small community the Catholic influence of the Spanish invasion had left in its wake a suspicion of—and therefore a repression of—the medicine teachings.

"There was a lot of oppression for medicine men back then," Amado recalled. "I was not allowed to talk about it with anybody, not even my own parents. My grandfather would always be very careful not to talk about it with anyone. The whole community knew him as a midwife, as a healer. But was he known as a keeper of a lineage? No. He had to keep it in secret. For a long time, these teachings almost only existed in legend, but in fact they had only gone into hiding. Recently, I have come to realize how all this could so easily have been lost and how it is being lost in many communities."

But, he said, with a smile, "There is a sacred time for everything, and now it is coming back. It is important that it is opening now because humanity is entering into a major transition when this wisdom will become essential."

Now in his late twenties, Amado had become a respected healer and teacher in his own right, so much so that he had recently been recognized as a member of his community's council of elders, an honor that had never been bestowed upon anyone as young as he. "Which is beautiful for me because it is honoring the youth," Amado later told me, with genuine humbleness. "It says that you are an elder when you are carrying wisdom and put it into service, not when you carry the years."

Amado's humbleness came in part from an awareness that this honor is one that he must continue to earn over a lifetime because, as he said, "The more years we carry, the heavier we become with all the mistakes that we have made. So when I am 40 years old, maybe I will not deserve to be on that council, because who knows what will happen in the next 10 years! I don't know. I don't know."

I hoped that Amado would have some ideas about how I should go about "looking for *yanantin*." I had been in Cuzco for only three days and I was already beginning to feel discouraged. During the first couple of days, as I reacquainted myself with the city by wandering around the markets, I asked several of the vendors (all native Andeans) what they knew about the term *yanantin*. My question was received with furrowed brows and strange looks and eventual embarrassment on both our parts. My host family had not heard of it either, though when I explained it further, one of them asked, "Oh! Like *yin yang*?" I made a mental note to ask Amado about this. If this idea of complementary opposites is such an important aspect of Andean cosmology, why did no one seem to know about it?

A small boy strolled up to me and asked if I wanted to buy postcards. I shook my head. "Please, *amiga*," he implored, and then, seeing that he had been spotted by one of the *policías turisticas*, stuffed the postcards into the front of his shirt and quickly moved away. A moment later, I spotted

Amado across the plaza. Amado's entire physical presence was proof of his indigenous ancestry. Like many native Andeans, he walked with a low center of gravity, making him appear like a *tirakuna*, an earth spirit who had just sprung up out of the ground. His face, high cheeked and angular, looked as if it had been carved out of dark marble. It was a face that could be carbon-dated back to the earliest inhabitants of this land.

"Amadocito!" I exclaimed, using the Spanish diminutive form of his name.

"¡Princesa!" he said, and swung me back and forth in his arms. I couldn't help but smile at being called *princesa*, a term of endearment used by Peruvian men for women they are fond of. What woman doesn't like to be thought of as a princess?[2]

Amado joined me on the bench. He asked how my flight was, how I liked the family that I was staying with. Good, good, all good, I told him. I asked after his wife and presented him with the gifts that I had brought for them. I asked Amado if Julián had ever seen a kangaroo, and Amado laughed when he saw it.

"Thaaaaank you, Princesa!"

There was a little more chitchat and then Amado said, "Tell me about your project."

Storm clouds were building from the east. The rainy season, which normally ends at the beginning of March, had extended later into the season. It rained for an hour almost every afternoon for the next month and a half I was there. Amado listened as I talked about my concern for the way Western philosophical models split the world into antagonistic pairs, my interest in the term *yanantin*, and my desire to understand how this complementary model of existence shapes the lives of those who still follow this perspective.

Eager to start this understanding right away, I did exactly what one of my mentors told me *not* to do when I asked her for advice on doing anthropological fieldwork. "Don't ask questions," she told me. "Just watch." But I asked anyway. I couldn't help myself. It was a kind of compulsion. I needed to bring home concrete data. What if I was there for the next month and a half and returned home with nothing to show for it?

"How would you define *yanantin*?" I asked Amado, pulling out a pen and opening my notebook to a fresh page.

Amado squinted up at the sky for a moment. And then, still staring upward, he said, "Out of respect I do not define *yanantin*."

"No?"

"No, I don't. All I know of it is its mystery. *Yanay. Warma yana.* In Quechua, it has millions of meanings."

But my inner academic would not be dissuaded. It wanted answers.

"Would you be willing to let me interview you?" I asked him.

"Yes, Princesa," he said, now turning to me with an amused look. "You can interview me if you want. But may I suggest that you download the information from the cosmos instead?"

Although I was trying to go with the flow, my inner academic wanted to weep. Download the information from the cosmos? What the hell did that mean? Why did he have to talk so cryptically? I nodded and stammered a hesitant "Yes, great," though in truth I didn't have a clue what he was talking about. I would get used to that feeling of cluelessness. Over the course of my time in Peru, there were times—many, many times, in fact—in which my Western cultural habits, biases, and presuppositions became embarrassingly apparent and felt like insurmountable roadblocks to understanding how Amado and the rest of my participants viewed the world. At these times, I became all too aware of my limitations and how deeply entrenched I was in the philosophical mind-set that I was trying so hard to leave behind.

Feeling disheartened, I finally owned up to my confusion.

"Okay . . . but . . . how exactly do I do that?"

"Ceremony."

Ceremony, he said, as if just that one word should make everything clear. Mercifully, before I had to ask, he elaborated. Amado had a friend named Juan Luis, a shaman who worked ceremonially with San Pedro, a mescaline-bearing cactus used for centuries as part of the healing rituals of northern Peru. If I wanted, they would take me up into the hills above Cuzco and, with the help of San Pedro, I would receive my first teaching.

"The Medicine will help you understand *yanantin*," Amado told me. "But not only that. It will help you *be yanantin*."

I had little experience with *entheogens* and many concerns. But Amado was reassuring.

"Juan Luis's preparation is gentle. And we will be there to guide you through. Don't worry, Princesa, you will be safe and you will learn so much from the spirit of San Pedrito."

Amado suggested that I talk to Juan Luis before deciding. We agreed to meet the next day.

After hugging Amado good-bye, I sat back down on the bench, reflecting on our conversation. *Download the information from the cosmos.* It was a beautiful phrase, one that sparked images of *Matrix*-like processes of understanding that do not need to be learned slowly over years or lifetimes but rather implies a kind of knowledge that is immediate and total. Revelation. Illumination. The kind of thing that I wanted to believe in, but on some level I was afraid to, for fear that I would discover, disappointed, that such things could not really be. At least not for me. That's what my culture of origin would have me believe anyway. It was what I had been trained in since birth. And even though I had been studying shamanic principles and techniques for several years before my fieldwork even began—during which time I had a number of profound experiences that created deep cracks in my Western-based paradigms—if I was to learn anything over the course of my fieldwork it was this: *Habits of mind are hard to break.*

This is especially true when it comes to altering one's epistemological premises—that is, one's cultural assumptions about the value of knowledge, how knowledge is attained, what constitutes "truth" and what is "illusion," and, based on these assumptions, determining what is "real" and what is "not real." Epistemology is at the root of a culture's conception of how the world "works." It acts as the foundation for how we see the world and therefore how we interact with it. Whether we realize it or not, in each moment we are making decisions concerning what we know, how we know it, and acting upon judgments about how we should proceed with that knowledge (Williams, 2005).

Because it plays such an important role within a culture's model of reality, trying to integrate the Andean epistemological system became one of my primary tasks during my time there. Given this, it was wonderfully appropriate that my first interaction with Amado turned a spotlight onto certain distinctions between the epistemological premises of our two worldviews.

My intense reaction to his suggestion that I "download the information from the cosmos" was highly revealing. Western culture is one of Ultimate Meanings, one more interested in understanding the universal than the particular. Our search for knowledge attempts to identify that which is unchanging across time, space, and within all states of consciousness. Western science and religion both have their roots in this same fundamental belief that there are universal standards and/or laws that are constant over time, over space, and that are independent of situation or circumstance. Ani (1994) wrote, "What is unknowable for the European causes anxiety. The European psyche needs the illusion of a rationally ordered universe in which everything can be known" (p. 63).

As I was to discover, for Amado and the rest of my Andean participants, there was much, much less energy spent trying to tease apart what constitutes Universal Truth. During one of our conversations, I asked Amado and Juan Luis how they determined what is real and what is unreal, what is truth and what is illusion.

Juan Luis said, "Everything is a reality and everything is a dream. Perhaps reality is a dream. And perhaps our dreams are our reality. We can say so much about it and still not have a complete understanding. What I can say is that what is real for me might not be real for another person. You would look at the people around you and know that each person is a cosmos. Each one has lived something different from the other. And what is most important is what each person has to teach. So why would we spend time finding out who has reasoning and who has not? What is real and what is not? It is better just to live life. No more. Just live."

Amado added, "Grandfather said that everything you believe, everything you know, everything you experience, is not really yours. Nothing that you think is happening within you is actually yours. It could be real for the person who is next to you, who is witnessing it. This is how we share realities. That is why there is such a truth when Juan Luis says that what is real for you is not real for the other person. That is exactly so. That is true for all levels—spiritual, physical, conscious, unconscious—all levels."

Apffel-Marglin (1998) suggested that the distinction between Western and Andean ways of knowing come down to knowledge based upon thought (Western) versus knowledge based upon experience (Andean). In the Quechua language, *yuyaysapa*, the closest word for *intelligence* or *intelligent*, more directly translates as "a person who has the capacity to remember and to put everything that he or she learns into practice."

As the shaman don Ignacio would later tell me, "The ancestors worked with simplicity. Wisdom was not about gaining all knowledge or much knowledge. They wanted less theory so that they could practice more. The practice of theory of the sacred knowledge . . . *that* was wisdom. They practiced it. I 'know' it because I am experiencing it. If I have so much knowledge and no time to practice it, then I know nothing. I only know about it. I don't really know it. That is why now we say it is time to *uneducate* ourselves. . . . After the practice, you can make your own theory."

This distinction is such an important aspect of the Andean model of reality that the Quechua language contains suffixes that distinguish between knowledge that has been experienced firsthand by the speaker and knowledge that is hearsay and/or removed from the speaker's firsthand experience (for example, historical or mythic stories). In other words, there is an emphasis on discriminating between information that one has a personal relationship to and information that one does not.

As I was to discover, the *relationship* between entities or energies is perhaps *the* essential component within Andean epistemology and, specifically, within the context of *yanantin*. In Western philosophy, and in particular in Western scientific thinking, what is "real" is determined by creating divisions between oneself and the phenomenon that one wishes to "know." In order to know, we must be detached, independent from the object of inquiry. The "thinking being" must dissociate himself or herself emotionally from the phenomenon or entity to be known in order to be objective, for only through objectivity can true knowledge be acquired. A methodological split is thus created between the knower and the known. The two become estranged. In the Andes, on the other hand, the world within and the world without is experienced phenomenally, through the interrelationship of the knower and that which one wants to know. True knowledge entails an exchange of energies, a dialogue of essences.

Just as relationships shift according to circumstance, truth likewise shifts. Nothing is static and nothing is absolute. Knowledge is therefore not accumulated and then transmitted from one person to another. One does not study and then "do." Rather, one engages with a subject and learns along the way, for only through interacting with the entity or energy, through *participating* with it, can one establish a relationship with it and come to know it. Fernandez (1998) wrote,

> Here in the Andes, we do not learn formally, seriously. We do not learn with instruction manuals or submit to didactic methods. Here we do everything our way. We learn to play the guitar familiarizing ourselves with the sounds of its chords and "talking out" little by little the songs that we like. We learn chess by watching

it being played until we know each piece's move, and then we just play. We do not take guitar lessons or buy chess manuals—we go directly to the toy we like and play with it. (p. 142)

During one of my visits, Amado mentioned that he wanted to speak Japanese.

"So you are going to study it?" I asked him.

He shook his head.

"No, I'm just going to start speaking it."

What a concept! Not to try to understand something by breaking it down into reducible parts and measured steps, but just to begin. I came to realize that this was the message that Amado was giving me that afternoon on the bench when he told me to "download" the information. Although at the time I could not fully grasp how knowledge could be acquired in this way, I did, at least on an intellectual level, understand that he was telling me that I needed to experience *yanantin* firsthand rather than try to understand it in a removed, detached way—for example, through concretized definitions. Although at the time I felt intellectual frustration at Amado's polite refusal to define *yanantin*, his refusal was, as he said, done "out of respect" for the fluid nature of the term. Over time, and with some hindsight, I came to recognize that his response told me more about the nature of *yanantin* than if he had given in to my request for a concrete and unchanging definition.

One day, seeing my frustration at my own lack of understanding regarding some of the concepts he was sharing with me, he said, "Something I have been noticing in people from the North is that I would hear a lot of them saying, 'Oh, that makes sense!' And they would be happy if it made sense. And I thought, wow, these people live so much in their mind! The mind is very powerful, so that's good. And then now I hear people saying, 'You know, that doesn't make sense!' And they are happy. So that liberation I celebrate. Because it doesn't have to make sense. That's pure wisdom to me. Because when you arrive to that nothingness it will not make sense!"

He started laughing and then said, "Imagine that! No thinking, no reasoning, not even feeling. None of that. Complete and absolute nothingness. Nothingness! Imagine that!"

"I can't," I responded, cringing at the slight whine in my voice.

"You can't imagine that? Then perhaps you need to experience it first. When you do, such a beautiful thing happens. Because when it has to make sense there is a lot of suffering."

Over time—and as the result of a series of illuminations, both beautiful and painful—I eventually began to loosen my tight, Western-based epistemological grip on the world and allowed things to "not make sense." Amado was right—there was a lot less suffering that way.

But the process of chipping away at some of my culture's engrained epistemological beliefs would only occur with time. It would only occur after a number of experiences with the phenomenon of *yanantin* forced me to push, sometimes painfully, through the boundaries of my Western thinking. Such revelations would come later. *Much* later. Sitting there on the bench in the plaza that day, watching Amado walk away, I felt nothing but lost and foolish and alone in my frustration and ignorance. I had come there to try to shift my consciousness, but in that moment I felt about as blind and stuck in my own limitations and cultural habits as I possibly could.

Thunder rumbled overhead. A moment later it started to rain. The children playing in the plaza squealed with delight. Tourists dashed for shelter. I got up from the bench and slipped on my rain jacket. I felt heavy then; lightness would come later.

FIGURE 4: © Carl A. Hyatt, 2010, Rope Bridge, Sicuani, Peru

CHAPTER TWO

Mind and Body; Spirit and Flesh

THE NEXT AFTERNOON, I returned to the plaza to meet Amado and Juan Luis. On my way, I cut through one of the tourist markets and once again tried to engage in conversation with some of the vendors about *yanantin*. Just as before, my questions were received with strange looks and even suspicious uncertainty.

As I approached the plaza, I found Amado and Juan Luis already standing near the fountain waiting for me.

I liked Juan Luis immediately. As I was to learn, he had a perpetually impish look on his face, making him look as if he was always about to tell the world's funniest—and *dirtiest*—joke. In fact, he often was. He laughed easily, the kind of laugh that seemed to bubble up from the depths of him and explode forth, like the carbonation in a bottle of soda that had been shaken and then opened suddenly. One got the impression that, once started, it might not be able to be contained. Just the sound of it would have me doubled over in laughter whether I understood what was being said or not. Unlike Amado, Juan Luis had the lighter skin and rounder features of a mestizo, a mix of indigenous and Spanish descent. His hair was curly and stuck out at all angles.

After we greeted each other with hugs and kisses, I followed Amado and Juan Luis up to one of the second-floor *balcónes* overlooking the square. Amado and Juan Luis each ordered a slice of apple cake and a *ponche de leche*—warm, sweetened milk mixed with pisco, a grape alcohol made in the Pisco region of Peru. Though delicious, I had learned on one of my previous trips to Peru that *ponche* goes down a little *too* easily and that the resulting hangover, combined with the altitude, felt like being kicked in the head by a llama. I ordered a *maté de coca* instead. Coca leaf is the most sacred plant among the indigenous highlanders of Peru and a component of almost all ceremonies as well as in divination practices and the diagnosing of illness. It is also a survival necessity for altitude-weary travelers. A mild stimulant similar to caffeine, it is common practice to ingest coca tea to alleviate altitude sickness.[1] Symptoms of altitude sickness, or *sorache*, vary from person to person. For me, it always included insomnia and headaches for the first few days after my arrival. The taste was pleasant, so I ordered *maté* every chance I got.

The waiter brought our drinks and then dashed back to get the cakes. I told Amado and Juan Luis about the strange reaction I seemed to get whenever I asked people about *yanantin*. They exchanged knowing looks. Juan Luis started to giggle and, trying to be polite, lowered his eyes and took a long drag of his *ponche* through the straw.

"Not everyone here knows about *yanantin*, Princesa," Amado said. "It is something that we were told to forget when colonization came in. We could not speak of it openly because, as you've heard, *yana* also means 'black,' and because of that, it was considered something dark. The Spanish saw it as the work of the devil, and therefore we were taught not to speak about it. That was part of the process of being disconnected from this philosophy."

"Also," he said with a small smile creeping onto his lips, "sometimes the word *yana* is used as slang to refer to genitalia. They might have thought you were trying to make a sexual joke."

"Or maybe they thought you were looking for a man!" Juan Luis piped up, with a wicked smile on his face.

Hearing this, my face turned bright red and I put my head in my hands.

"Oh, sweet Jesus," I moaned.

Amado and Juan Luis burst into laughter. The Danish tourists sitting at the next table turned to look at us. The next five minutes were devoted to Amado and Juan Luis acting out a scene in which they imagined me going around asking people about their *yanantins*.

"Next time you should say *yanantin-masintin* rather than just *yanantin*," Amado advised me.

"Why is that?"

"As I said yesterday, *yanantin* is defined in thousands of ways, no? Yet, I will say that it does involve the relationship, the alliance, the meeting, and the unity between two beings. Two beings. Not necessarily humans. *Beings.* But where it becomes very powerful and why it is used on the path of the medicine people is when you use the word *masintin* with it. This is where both of these beings come together in absolute service, in absolute mission together. *Masintin* is where the power of the two become the force that will allow whatever that these *yanantin* are dreaming to manifest."

"Could you say a little more about that?" I asked him.

"The *masintin* part, to me, is what makes the *yanantin* relationship real," he said. "*Masintin* is the process, the experience of that *yanantin* relationship. That is why *masintin* is important in *yanantin*. It's the fun part! Pretty cool, huh? It is still *yanantin*, but with *masintin*, it's fun!"

I thought about this for a moment.

"So," I said slowly, "would you say that *yanantin* is kind of like the noun; the relationship as it is but static in and of itself? And then that *masintin* is like the verb, the action, the energetic unfolding that occurs between the *yanantin* pair?"

"Yes! Let's say that *masintin* is the verb. I love it. *Being* is *yanantin*. *Masintin* is the *experience*. *Yanantin* exists already. Only with *masintin* can you get through the process."

Later, the shaman don Ignacio would make a similar distinction between *yanantin* and *masintin* when he said, "*Masintin* is what is materialized. It is what is self-realized, not what stays in theory. *Masintin* is to enter into the spirit and the essence of anything, of the thing. Of what has been materialized. Of what has been imagined. You must enter into the spirit of it. *Masintin* is to create, recreate, and procreate."

I turned to Juan Luis and told him about the research that I was there to do. "How would you suggest I try to understand *yanantin*?" I asked him.

Juan Luis said something quietly to Amado. Amado nodded. Juan Luis turned to me and said, "Amado has said this to you and I would like to suggest it as well, that you come into ceremony with us and work with San Pedro, with the Medicine. This is the best way for you to understand *yanantin*."

The San Pedro plant (*Trichocereus pachanoi*) is a tall, columnar, mescaline-bearing cactus that grows in the hot sandy soil of the coastal desert of northern Peru. It is typically prepared as a liquid, the meat of the cactus boiled with water into a thick liquid so that the mescaline content—the vision-inducing ingredient—is highly concentrated. The result is a mucilaginous and highly bitter drink. As has been reported by Joralemon and Sharon (1993), the ritual use of San Pedro is one of the main tools of the *curanderos* of northern Peru, who use the hallucinogenic substance ritually by either giving it to their patients, taking it themselves, or both. In this altered state, the *curandero* is able to diagnose an illness and then confront the spirit causing it. Sharon (1972) wrote,

> [The] San Pedro cactus is experienced as the catalyst that enables the curandero to transcend the limitations placed on ordinary mortals, to activate all his senses; project his spirit or soul; ascend and descend into the supernatural realms ... [to] "jump over" barriers of time, space, and matter; divine the past, present, and future—in short, to attain vision, "to see." (p. 130)

Don Ignacio told me one night, "When you give yourself fully to the master plant and to allow that through our nature, of our cosmos in macro and micro levels, of this world, of the physical temple, of the *ukhu pacha* which is the inner temple of the mental or the psychological and of that vital energy or also called spirit. Through those three temples or levels may flow everything. To let it flow. . . . That essence is what will allow us to understand deeper and in a more profound way in the heart and from the heart. Not only from our mind. There has to be a strategic alliance between the power of the mind that creates, recreates, and procreates constantly and love from the heart. That way we can think in a loving way and we will feel creatively, creating and recreating and procreating new life of light."

He continued. "Many people call it drugs. They call it a 'hallucinogen.' I have many lifetimes with this Medicine. And this lifetime, I have 35 years.

In that time, I have not hallucinated once. But my vision has been opened many times."

It is hard to explain why I did not immediately jump at Juan Luis's invitation. At first, I assumed that my resistance was just an extension of the epistemological doubt that I had felt the day before—a skepticism that I could gain any "true" insight that would extend past what I felt would be the dubious insight of a drug-induced haze. My intellectual distrust was a part of it, to be sure. Epistemological doubt is, after all, part of my cultural inheritance. But now, with Amado and Juan Luis looking at me, waiting for my answer, I had to admit that it was not just skepticism that was at the base of my discomfort. It was fear.

Fear of what exactly? Fear of losing control of my mind, I supposed. A dread of what might happen if I did. In general, Western culture is mistrustful of altered states of consciousness, of anything that takes us out of our "ordinary" epistemological framework and into nonordinary states of awareness. This, too, is my cultural inheritance.

In their often-cited study, linguists Lakoff and Johnson (1980) considered how the language with which we are raised reveals our unconscious relationships to ourselves and the world around us. They highlighted metaphors inherent in the English language through which we make meaning about our world. For example, they present the metaphor of "The Mind is a Brittle Object" as reflective of how we experience psychological states, as in "the experience *shattered* him," "her ego is very *fragile*," and "his mind *snapped*" (p. 28).

The mind is a brittle object. With this image lodged in our unconscious, no wonder we have such a hard time letting go of our hold on consensus reality! Things that are brittle shatter into hundreds of tiny pieces and can never be repaired; or, if they can be, it is a tenuous kind of repair, and even when made whole again, the ruptures remain painfully visible. Nothing returns to its original structural integrity after being shattered. Given this, we hold on tight to our sense of "control" over the mind, for if we lose our firm grip on standardized meaning, what then? We risk madness, alienation, loneliness, and the antagonism of a world that we now do not understand and that does not understand us, for it only recognizes one way of relating to existence. ("And even that way is hardly understood," Amado later commented.)

My apprehension of going into ceremony with Amado and Juan Luis reflected these cultural presumptions upon which I had been raised.

Specifically, it butted up against my culture's basic understanding of what consciousness is, what role it plays in the world, and its inherent fragility. Although I liked to believe that my years of spiritual and psychological practice had given me a certain confidence in the workings of my own mind and psyche, faced with this opportunity that Amado and Juan Luis were presenting me, I also had to acknowledge my own anxiety concerning what I might discover within my psyche. No matter how much inner work I had done in the past, I had no doubt that there were things about myself that I did not know, things hidden around the corners of my consciousness that might emerge and destroy me on some fundamental level. What dark thoughts that usually lie hidden within its depths might be let loose? I had not realized before this just how much that metaphor of the mind as a "brittle object" had affected my relationship to my own mind.

As I was to learn, Andean philosophical models do not perceive the mind or spirit or soul as being brittle. Nor is the spirit/mind/consciousness considered an "object"—that is, something solid and rigid. Rather, consciousness is believed to be able to shapeshift into multiple forms and multiple states. There is the sense that consciousness can participate with the rest of the world in a way that dissolves the boundaries between things while still maintaining its individual integrity. Thus, in the Andean world, the desire to make shifts in consciousness is not suspect but, on the contrary, is considered essential to health and wholeness. In fact, the primary function of the Andean shaman is to create opportunities through ritual in which shifts in consciousness can be made that allow for a *yanantin* relationship to return to a balance through the process of creation, recreation, and procreation of energies.

The means by which this balancing occurs is through *ayni*, a Quechua word that loosely translates as *reciprocity*. Cultures modeled on philosophical systems of complementary dualism are distinguished by their emphasis on cooperation and institutionalized reciprocity. Likewise, the indigenous Andean way of life is based on the idea that life regenerates itself through mutual nurturance and aid. Indigenous Andeans (particularly those living in harsh mountainous environments) rely upon social and spiritual practices that promote cooperation and respect, for only through communal cooperation and a mutual exchange of services can life endure. Scholars have pointed out that *ayni* is "the hallmark of Andean life" (Bolin, 2006, p. 152) and that, as a result, "It is not possible to understand Andean life outside of *ayni*. Life itself is *ayni*" (Vasquez, 1998, p. 108). Or, as Allen (1988) put it,

> [a]t the most abstract level, ayni is the basic give-and-take that governs the universal circulation of vitality. It can be positive, as when brothers-in-law labour in each other's fields; or it can be negative, as when the two men quarrel and exchange insults. This circulation—be it of water or human energy—is driven by a system of continuous reciprocal interchanges. (p. 93)

Amado emphasized that the need for *ayni* does not just apply to relationships between one human being and another. Just as importantly, *ayni* must take place between human beings and the land, between human beings and the animals that they tend, and between human beings and the unseen forces of the three levels of reality that constitute the Andean cosmos.

According to the Andean cosmovision, existence is brought into being and kept in harmony through the *ayni* or reciprocal exchange between two *yanantin* energies. *Sami* is a light and refined energy, while *hucha* is a dense, heavy energy (Allen, 1988, 2002; Joralemon & Sharon, 1993; Wilcox, 1999). These complementary energies flow between the three levels of reality that constitute the Andean cosmos, in which a variety of spiritual energies exist: the *hanaq pacha*, the *kay pacha*, and the *ukhu pacha*[2] (Barnes, 1992; Bastien, 1992; Dover, 1992; Howard-Malverde, 1997; Seibold, 1992; Urton, 1981; Wilcox, 1999).

The *hanaq pacha*[3] is the upper world and is associated with God, the sun, the moon, and souls of the dead (Seibold, 1992). Amado described it as "the world of the stars, the world of the sun, the world of the moon. [It is] the world of the sky, the clouds, gods, the rainbow, the lightning, the thunder, and the stars that represent our brothers and sisters." The symbol of this realm is the condor. Wilcox (1999) reported that according to the Q'ero people of the highland Andes, the *hanaq pacha* is made up entirely of *sami* energy. Because *sami* is the energy responsible for creating harmony and proper connection with the rest of the cosmos, it is believed that the beings existing in the *hanaq pacha* always act in perfect *ayni*.

The *kay pacha*[4] is the middle, physical world of being. It is here that we humans exist, along with the animating energies of the natural world. The *kay pacha*, Amado told me, "is ruled by the puma, which represents the strength and the courage and the power of the people that have come into this world. It represents the path of the warrior. The important deities of the mountains, Pachamama, the rocks, the trees, mountains, *huacas*, the lakes—all of these represent the *kay pacha*. In the *kay pacha*, you have to work honoring all the land, honoring all the deities, taking care of Mother Earth, receiving all her gifts, giving back offerings for all that we received. This is the *kay pacha*. This life."

Wilcox (1999) reported that the *kay pacha* is composed of both *sami* and *hucha* energies, and that because the *kay pacha* is made up of both light and heavy energies, beings inhabiting this middle realm are in a constant interchange of *sami* and *hucha*. Therefore, those of us existing in the *kay pacha* sometimes act in *ayni* and sometimes do not. Amado told me that at our current level of consciousness, *hucha* cannot be avoided, that it is an inevitable product of living in the *kay pacha*.

Scholars most often refer to the *ukhu pacha*[5] as the "underworld" (Barnes, 1992; Bastien, 1992; Dover, 1992; Seibold, 1992; Wilcox, 1999), though some scholars (Urton, 1981; Platt, 1997) have translated it as "inner world" or "interior place." Urton (1981) reported that the *kay pacha* and *ukhu pacha* are mirror images of one another and that in the *ukhu pacha*, "everything happens just the opposite to the way it happens on this earth; our sunrise is their sunset, our day is their night, and our earth is their sky" (Urton, 1981, p. 38). Amado emphasized the latter definition of "inner world," saying that to call it an "underworld" or even "lower world" is incorrect, a mistranslation. Rather, he said, it means "deep within" and "the place where life is being born." The *ukhu pacha* is symbolized by the *amaru*, or serpent. Wilcox (1999) reported that the *ukhu pacha* is made up entirely of *hucha* because the beings there have not yet learned how to live in *ayni*.

Although often mistakenly associated with the Christian "hell," indigenous Andeans do not consider the *ukhu pacha* (or the *hucha* energy associated with it) to be intrinsically bad or evil. On the contrary, the heavy energy of *hucha* is both necessary and transformative when kept in balance with its energetic counterpart, *sami*. Mental or physical sickness is thus not perceived as being due to an evil spirit such as the Christian devil but is considered to be the result of a breakdown in reciprocity between various energies (Joralemon & Sharon, 1993; Silverblatt, 1987, Wilcox, 1999). Silverblatt (1987) stated,

If we analyze pre-Columbian concepts of sickness . . . we discover that Andeans never define disease in terms of complots made with evil forces. Rather, concepts of disease and health were intrinsically related to a normative structure in which the maintenance of "balance" (*ayni*) between social, natural, and supernatural forces was a predominant ideal. Sickness was perceived to be a product of the breakdown of cultural norms regulating the balance between social groups, between society and nature, and between society and supernatural forces. (p. 173)

As individuals living in the *kay pacha*, human beings are in a constant interchange of *sami* and *hucha*, heavy and light energies. Illness is believed to occur when there is an excess of *hucha* energy built up within a system, which "turns the lightness of our energy body heavy like itself" (Wilcox, 1999, p. 31).

"We take on *hucha* from our families, community, friends—even from certain places on the planet," Amado said. "The cool thing is, we do the same with *sami*. The secret was to be getting lots of *sami* constantly and liberating the *hucha* if you can by transforming it. That is the service of the medicine man. That is the function of ritual."

Indeed, maintaining balance and harmony between the various facets of existence necessitates individuals who are adept at "mediating" between—or, as Platt (1986) suggested, "paring"—these opposing energies. In the high Andes of Peru, the task of equalizing *sami* and *hucha* energies in order to create a complementary balance falls upon healers and ritual specialists known as *paqos* (Allen, 1988, 2002; Bolin, 2006; Fernandez & Gutierrez, 1996; Glass-Coffin, 2004; Heckman, 2003; Urton, 1981; Webb, 2007; Wilcox, 1999). In other areas, such as the north coastal region of Peru, they are men and women referred to, respectively, as *curanderos* or *curanderas* (Glass-Coffin, 1998, 2004; Joralemon & Sharon, 1993). The primary task of the Andean shaman is to bring balance and health to the individual and community by determining the cause of the imbalance and working ritually to remove blockages and reestablish the flow of *ayni* between the various energies of existence and therefore create opportunities for healing (Webb, 2007). Heckman (2003) stated, "A fundamental belief underlying animism is that energy exists in all things—what we might call the life force—that needs to be maintained in a balanced state.

When the energy becomes unbalanced, rituals are required to regain equilibrium" (p. 113).

When I asked Amado about this idea, he emphasized that blockages are often the result of the mind's insistence on separating these interrelated systems in a way that they can no longer engage in a reciprocal exchange with one another. "Everything is interwoven," he said. "If you see the three worlds as separated, you have created blockages. According to my personal experience, people have forgotten that at all times we are in these three worlds. They are all connected energetically. What happens in the *ukhu pacha* also happens in those two other levels. All of the three worlds are related to the various activities of our lives. Like, for example, different aspects of the moon—which is the *hanaq pacha*—determine how our harvest is going to be, how our seeding time is going to be. Is the land fertile yet? Or not yet? Nowadays there's so much disconnection and blockage that we cannot experience the two other levels. But as soon as you realize that really they are not separated, the blockages disappear. So, for a healing to work, we have to begin inside our hearts. We must acknowledge and honor that we cannot separate them, because they are all the same. When we are doing ceremony, that is what we are doing—opening the gates [between the three worlds] so that they can be linked again. It is not any more that we can have them open at all times. When we are doing a healing with the person we say, 'Spirits of the *hanaq pacha, ukhu pacha, kay pacha*, help and guide this person, wherever this person is.' A long time ago, my grandfather could say, 'All the spirits of this land, support and guide this person whether this person is in the *hanaq pacha, ukhu pacha*, or *kay pacha.*' See? Totally different. Because back then we could access these levels so easily. But now, these three levels have to be opened because the gates are closed."

Amado continued, "Something very interesting to say about the three different worlds is that they are related to our physical bodies. When we walk, one step, the other step, as we put one foot here and another foot there, there is an energy line that goes to the next one. And then there is another energy line that goes to the next one. So, we walk the path of the serpent. So, that is our *ukhu pacha* level, from our knees below. From our knees up higher is the energy of the puma, the power of taking care of and experiencing this world, the *kay pacha.*"

He patted his belly.

"For example," Amado said, "all of the heavy energy is digested here, all of our food is digested here. All the things that come in this life, whether it is fear, whether it is cold, whether it is heat, anything is experienced here in this area, in the area of the puma. The power of our heart is representing the courage of the warrior, of the puma."[6]

Amado then brought his hands up to his eyes.

"And then, here, our eyes, seeing the bigger picture, our ability to be up higher, with far vision like the condor. To see the unseen. And like the condor, in one flight to live a lifetime, to see a lifetime. To be able to connect to the condor means we can experience lifetimes."[7]

One of the most enduring debates in the history of Western philosophy surrounds the question of which—the mind or the body, the spirit or the flesh—is most real and unchanging and therefore "true." This conundrum has been referred to as the "mind-body problem." Likewise, in the field of consciousness studies, philosophers and scientists struggle with the so-called "hard problem" of consciousness (Chalmers, 1995), hoping to explain how these two seemingly disparate elements of the human experience—the physical brain and our resulting subjective experience—"link up" in order to create the human experience. Not being able to prove how this occurs, in the Western world, mind and body coexist, but begrudgingly and in separate domains. This constitutes a "problem" according to our worldview and, according to Amado, creates blockages that result in imbalance.

At dinner one night, Juan Luis and I discussed the Western world's perceived "problem" of consciousness versus the way it is viewed in Andean terms.

"Here, those things are two," Juan Luis said, spreading his fingers apart in a V, "and, they are one," he then said, bringing his fingers together. He then shrugged. "There is no problem."

Allen (2002) wrote,

> The sensual incompatibility between Christianity and indigenous beliefs lies in the different understandings of the relationship between body and soul. The Andean worldview does not accommodate the Western dualism of body and soul; for Andeans, all matter is in some sense alive, and conversely, all life has a material base. (p. 44)

The waiter came with our apple cakes. My head was gently throbbing and I took another sip of coca tea. According to Amado, for a healing to work, a shift in consciousness must occur in order for these blockages to be dissolved, through which an exchange of *ayni* can take place, and a *yanantin* relationship can unfold. But what would it take for a Westerner such as myself to be able to disrupt my usual patterns of thinking and dissolve these blockages? This, it seemed, was what was being asked of me if I was going to understand *yanantin* at the level that I wanted to. Sitting there in the restaurant, I knew that if I were to have a chance at understanding *yanantin*, I would have to find ways of experiencing this dissolution of boundaries. To do so, I had to overcome the fear that had created the separation and antagonism to begin with.

But this was easier said than done. Fear is, after all, the ego's most reliable hiding place. And so I hesitated.

"I guess I still need to think about it," I said, on some level hating myself, feeling like a coward.

"Of course, Princesa," Amado said. "You decide."

"In the meantime," he said, standing up suddenly, "there's something I want to show you."

FIGURE 5: © Carl A. Hyatt, 2005, Interdimensional Doorway, Bolivia

CHAPTER THREE

Of Time and Space

A LONG THE SOUTHEAST SIDE of Avenida del Sol ("Avenue of the Sun"), not far from the Plaza de Armas, is a 150-foot mural upon which is painted a pictorial representation of the history of Cuzco. Within the boundaries of the mural, illustrations of the city's past, present, and imagined future roll into one another seamlessly, beginning with images of pre-Columbian times, then transitioning into scenes of the Inca reign, including the sun-honoring festival Inti Raymi. These more joyous images are replaced by brutal scenes of the torture and cultural decimation that took place during the Spanish invasion in the sixteenth century. The next section of the mural shows the Andean people's resistance to the European invaders, including the battle at the great stone fortress of Sacsayhuaman that overlooks the city. The final portion of the mural shows Peru's independence from the Spanish in 1821. Here, a group of Cusqueños looks off into the distance, their arms thrown up in joy and optimism. They stand on Inca stonework—a symbol of the literal and figurative foundation of their great city. At the foremost section of the mural, closest to the viewer's gaze, a high-cheeked Inca dives forward into the future. The next section of the mural, it is implied, will be entirely his.

As well as being a chronicle of Cuzco's history, the Avenida del Sol mural reflects a prophesy that at some time in the future the *runa* (indigenous Andeans) will return to power and regain their position as masters of the land (Allen, 2002), establishing "an age of plenty and social harmony" (Classen, 1993, p. 143).

Standing at the mural's center is a depiction of Pachacuteq, the ninth Inca king-hero, whose name translates to "he who turns time-space" (Sullivan, 1988, p. 174). Pachacuteq is honored for having expanded the Inca civilization not only geographically but also spiritually. Amado told me, "He was a leader, a great governor, a prophet, and also a great and powerful healer."

It is from his name that the Andean people get the word *pachacuti*, which is used to describe a mytho-historical event of great significance. In Quechua, the prefix *pacha-* represents both time and space *simultaneously* (Urton, 1981). Cruz (2007) said that in the Andes, "[time and space] cannot be separated. . . . They are like two faces of the same coin. You cannot separate one from the other because the *pacha* is time, but it is also space" (n.p.).

The widespread use of the word *pacha* in the Quechua language is noteworthy. Used alone, the word has multiple, yet interrelated, meanings. It can refer to a group of related entities (both human and nonhuman) existing in a similar geographic area (Apffel-Marglin, 1998). As noted previously, the Andean cosmos is likewise split into three separate, yet interrelated, *pachas*—the *kay pacha*, the *ukhu pacha*, and the *hanaq pacha*. The term *Pachamama*, while often seen as being equivalent to what we in the West would refer to as Mother Earth, is viewed as a multidimensional entity or energy that is both physically present and contained within time.

The word *pacha* is also used to connote certain epochs in history. According to the Andean mythos, the history of the world is made up of a series of 500-year intervals of time called *pachas* (Allen, 2002). At the end of each 500-year cycle, it is said that the existing *pacha* ends and a new one begins. The transition time between the *pachas* is called a *pachacuti* (Allen, 2002; Classen, 1993; MacCormick, 1991; Sullivan, 1988; Urton, 1999; Wilcox, 1999). The word *cuti* translates as "revolution" or "turning over/around" (Urton, 1999, p. 41), and it is said that as one *pacha* or epoch replaces another, a "world reversal" occurs in which existence is turned inside out, thus revealing its opposite (Allen, 2002; MacCormick, 1991; Sullivan, 1988). In Quechua, the term *pachacuti* is said to mean "the world is transformed" (José Imbelloni, as cited in Sullivan, 1988, p. 878). In the Aymara language of Bolivia, it translates as "like a time of war" (according to Bertonio, as cited in Sullivan, 1988, p. 878). MacCormick (1991) described a *pachacuti* as a time when "what is up goes under and what is under comes up" (as cited in Heckman, 2003, p. 155). Sullivan (1988) likewise reflected that a *pachacuti* is a process in which "the world is overturned and set upside down" (p. 588). Urton (1999) reported that it is said that during this transition, time and space reverse themselves.

Although this may sound apocalyptic, it has been noted that while the movement from one epoch to another may include a certain amount of suffering (as any change invariably does), a *pachacuti* does not signal the absolute end of everything; rather, a *pachacuti* is considered a "cyclical cleansing and return" (Heckman, 2003, p. 155). It is a creational event, a time of transition from one age to another, in which one world is destroyed so that another can be born in its place. Each new world begins as a result of the cataclysmic destruction of the previous world and will itself end in a cataclysm so that a new *pacha* can emerge.

This transition is likewise the product of a *yanantin* relationship, for a *pachacuti* occurs when contradictory states of being initiate a transformation from one mode to its opposite. The rainy season gives way to the dry season. The dark of night becomes the light of day, and vice versa. Though we may not always like it, birth and death engage in a continual exchange of *ayni*. Sullivan (1988) noted, "Cycles are the product of the encounter between two unlike temporal modes. . . . Each cycle embraces contradictory states of being, [thus] allowing mutually exclusive states to coexist in an integral experience" (pp. 626–627).

"To me it is a return of the essence," Amado reflected when I asked him about the term. "It is a return of the soul. Especially when we are speaking about *yanantin*, *pachacuti* for me is the coming back of the highly enlightened and highly evolved soul—not only into humanity but also into all areas of life on our planet. It is not necessarily a reverse, but it is definitely a huge transition. It is a return of a certain essence that will bring the transformation to our planet that we need. *Pachacuti* for me is the return of that great soul."

During my fieldwork, several of my participants pointed out to me that understanding the Andean view of time and space as cyclical rather than linear is key to understanding the Andean complementary worldview. One evening, my Spanish teacher invited me to her house to meet her brother, a professor at a local university who was also interested in Peru's indigenous philosophies. While reserved at first, when I asked him about *yanantin*, he became quite animated. He said, "If you want to understand the mentality of the Andes, the most important thing to understand is our concept of time as cyclic. It is a mentality of spirals, not lines. For the Westerners, time is a line. In the Andes, it is a spiral."

"Why a spiral and not a circle?" I asked.

"A spiral is a circle that repeats," he answered.

Seeing the confusion on my face, he quoted a phrase from Eliade's (1954/1959) *Cosmos and History: The Myth of the Eternal Return*. "'To live in eternity,'" he said. He repeated it again, more slowly this time. "'To live in eternity.' That is the key. You see, with the idea of linear time comes history. Eliade spoke of this. Birth. Death. History is a line with no going backwards, only forwards. But in a spiral you can go forwards *and* backwards. It repeats. It renews. It is reversible. Within that spiral you can renew yourself. You can renew the world. Infinitely."

"A spiral," he said again, locking eyes with me, as if to make sure that I understood.

When I mentioned this discussion to Amado later, he had a slightly different take on this idea. "Actually," he said, "I would say that we understand both the linear and the cyclical. Linear time is how we access the future, through divination. That is how we know what the future will bring or how the past is influencing us. All that is accessible through linear time. Being linear isn't bad, it's just limited. When we are very linear, we don't really live in the now. When you are very linear, you have to be always ahead or behind. Pachamama brings you back to the cycle or the spiral. Because she is all about cycles and the cycle brings you to the here and now."

Ani (1994) wrote,

Lineal time fails spirituality. It pushes us constantly towards anxiety and fear. The European is always asking him/her self, even while he/she rests: Where am I going? What will become of me? Lineal time is one-dimensional because it has neither depth nor breadth, only the illusion of length. It leads to evolutionary theories. Reality is perceived as the continuous development of one entity through necessarily temporal stages. One stage is more "evolutionarily advanced" than the one it follows, since they are arranged or "unfold" in a temporal sequence. The concept is based on assumed lineal connections. (p. 61)

While the Andean cyclical/spiral model conceives of time as dynamic, not static, made up of alternating movements, the linear nature of Western consciousness brings with it a teleological focus, a focus on the achievement of some ultimate endpoint, which would result in the end of history once and for all. This endpoint is often conceived of as a moment in which some sort of perfection and freedom from the multiplicity of forms is achieved.

Tarnas (1991) wrote,

Perhaps the most pervasive and specifically Judaeo-Christian component tacitly retained in the modern world view was the belief in man's linear historical process toward ultimate fulfillment. Modern man's self-understanding was emphatically teleological, with humanity seen as moving in a historical development out of the darker past characterized by ignorance, primitiveness, poverty, suffering, and oppression, and toward a brighter ideal future characterized by intelligence, sophistication, prosperity, happiness, and freedom. (p. 321)

A movement toward ultimate fulfillment. Self-understanding as a teleological march out of ignorance toward an idealized future. Yes. That seemed to be the crux of the linear worldview—time as a unidirectional progression from lesser forms of consciousness to more evolved states. In Western thinking, we are always chasing utopias, hoping to get there through evolution, through progress, looking at where we currently are as inferior to some future state. But, as it has been pointed out, this kind of thinking is alien in Andean philosophical models, a worldview that rejects a linear evolutionist vision of the future. Cruz (2007) noted that in Andean thinking there is no concept of a messiah who brings with him an end to history. Likewise, Vasquez (1998) wrote, "It would not occur to anyone in the Andes to be considered civilized today and call their ancestors barbarians or savages, and thus discover a non-civilized type of human kinship" (p. 96).

Amado said, "That's why in the Andes we don't have a creation story, because creation is happening constantly, every day."

After saying good-bye to Juan Luis, Amado and I left the restaurant. We made our way across the plaza to his car. From there we sped up the mountain road out of town, dodging stray dogs and small children as we went. Along the way we passed the Inca fortress of Sacsayhuaman and the multitude of tourists crowding around the giant stone structure. About a half a mile later, Amado pulled the car over to the side of the road and hopped out.

"Come, Princesa! Come!" Amado called as he took off across the grass toward a large outcropping of rock in the distance. I was breathing heavily by the time I caught up to him. Amado put out his hand and helped me up onto the rock. Smiling broadly, he threw his arms open wide.

"This is all about *yanantin*," he told me. "Many people believe that this place is from Inca times, but I believe that it was created well before then. But look! Erosion had not faded it. It's remarkable."

I looked around. "What is?" I said.

Had he not been with me, pointing it out, I am sure I never would have seen the figures carved into the stone surface. But there they were. Once seen, it was impossible to unsee them. On each side of the rock, one on the right and one on the left, were the outline of two pumas. Between the pumas were two birds. Above and below these images were two snakes. The carvings were raised above the surface of the rock, in some ways easier to feel than to see.

"These carvings are believed to be part of a prophecy," Amado told me. "The puma on the left . . . there, see? That represents the North. The North— Canada, the United States, and the northern part of Mexico. For us, those areas of the world represent the power of 'Will' and 'Transformation.' And also 'Control' and the taking of resources. North Puma is said to be unconscious. It is sleeping. Sleeping is considered very sacred here. Sometimes only when you are asleep are you in complete connection with all the energies. And look at its belly! It is pregnant! It is pregnant, so it must sleep in order to wake up. When it wakes up, it will be capable of anything, any transformation. When it wakes up, North Puma will change the planet."

He pointed to the other puma, the one on the right.

"This one represents the South, as in South America," he said. "The puma of the South is the young puma, while the puma of the North is old. South Puma is the warrior. It is protecting Pachamama. South Puma can't do anything to wake up North Puma, but eventually North Puma will come to a point where it will have no choice but to recognize and accept its capacities."

"What capacities?"

"To bring change to the world. To bring *pachacuti* to the world. That's the main capacity I am talking about. Because already we know how the North and especially the United States affects the whole world. Anything that is done, anything that is said, arrives even to the most hidden corners of our planet. Fashion, music, English, the American dream . . . anything. So whatever happens in the North will also arrive not only in the shape of fashion or American culture but also in energy. That's the power this place has. It's a hub. It's a concentration. It's a vortex of energy for the whole planet. For that reason, it is said that when North Puma wakes up, even the color of the sky will change."

"Waking up is painful," I said.

"Definitely," Amado replied. "Especially when you have to give birth right after you wake up."

He pointed at the two birds. "That one is a condor and the other is an eagle. You can tell the difference between them because the wings of the eagle point backwards, while the wings of the condor are straight. The eagle represents the North and the condor the South. The prophecy says that the condor and the eagle always fly together. Always. Like now, with this process that you and I are doing together."

He moved around the rock to get an alternate view. "Then there are two serpents.[1] The one for the South is rooted in Pachamama and has such respect for Pachamama. My people are in love with Mother Earth and love doing ceremonies and offerings. The serpent on the left represents the North. It's longer than the other. See? The serpent of the North is not coming from Mother Earth. Instead, the North Serpent represents the inner world. It represents consciousness and things psychological. Even in the indigenous communities of the North, the Native Americans, only speak a little about Mother Earth. Most focused on is Great Spirit. But here, first is Mother Earth. First is Pachamama."

"What's the relationship of this place to *yanantin*?" I asked Amado.

"North and South," he said. "We belong to one spirit; one source. That is the message of this prophesy. It doesn't matter whether the puma of the

North wakes up or if the puma of the South goes to sleep. The condor and the eagle will always fly together. Always they are *yanantin* first and last. Through this we are told that we always have an ally. The moment we are born into this life, we are born into this life with a *yanantin*, at that soul level. That's a beautiful image for me—that although I can feel weak, or I can make mistakes, or I can be unevolved, or sleepy, or whatever, on a deeper level of my essence in spirit, in my connection to God, I am always flying with my *yanantin*. Always. That's like . . . ahhh . . . beautiful! Our *yanantin* always exists. Not only for humanity, but also for all beings of life, in all dimensions of life."

"This prophesy, then, is about a *pachacuti*?" I asked.

"To me, the *pachacuti* is about the awakening of the North Puma. Because in the South we are perfect!" He laughed and then shook his head. "No, no . . . Not really. The *pachacuti* will affect everybody—both condor and eagle, both pumas, both serpents. There is always a next level. For us as well. I don't know if I told you this but I was wondering if maybe one day people in the North will be so awake and so connected to ceremony that people here in the South will forget about that and focus on something else. If the *pachacuti* will mean a time of us falling asleep while you all in the North are awake. Perhaps we are just temporary guardians of this wisdom and philosophy and lineages and traditions."

"I suppose that makes sense," I said. "If in a *yanantin* pair the two never become exactly alike, then one always picks up where the other leaves off. If a *pachacuti* is a 'world reversal,' then perhaps one turns into the other."

"Yes, when you think of a reversal, it's like people who were awake go to sleep and people who were asleep wake up. And yet in the type of *pachacuti* that I connect with—where there is the return of that essence—nobody goes to sleep. That essence returns and everybody wakes up."

"What happens when everybody is finally awake?" I wanted to know.

"We party!" he said. "The cool thing is that a *pachacuti* doesn't have to be a hard process. It *can* be—and if it can be it will be—but it doesn't have to be. It doesn't have to be a hard process. It is up to the person."

"I don't know," I said, shaking my head. "Human beings don't tend to take change all that well. At least not where I come from."

"But, in fact, humanity has the most powerful capacity to adapt," Amado said. "We are ready to live through glaciers and even through global warming and all of that. The thing is, we don't use all our capacities until we need them There's just no will, there's just no desire, there's just no initiative to use these capacities beforehand, to prevent. We just use it when we need it. That's when it comes out the most. So, we are waiting until something more intense happens, and then we will use these capacities to connect, to adapt, to wake up and everything. At that point, it is not a choice anymore. You do . . . or you do. And those who are able to become absolutely harmonized and absolutely connected will adapt."

"Aren't we supposedly in the midst of a *pachacuti* right now?" I asked him.

"The belief is that we are right now in preparation for a major transition. The Q'ero people refer to this time as the *taripay pacha*. The *taripay pacha* is a very powerful time. *Taripay pacha* is grammatically translated as 'the future.' It's not ahead of you, it's behind you. That's why you can't see it. You see, in the Andes we believe that our future is not ahead of us but is behind us. The past goes ahead of you. The past is what has passed. That's why the word *past* in Quechua means 'in front.' Therefore, the future must catch up with us. It must catch up with our reality. So, the *taripay pacha* represents a time and a space that is catching up with you. You can't see it, you can't perceive it. But it will reach you eventually."

"That's an interesting way to put it. Time is catching up to us, rather than us being dragged along by time, rather than us being victims of time."

"Totally. *Taripay pacha* is a time to meet with ourselves, because it represents absolute awakened consciousness; the return of this highly evolved soul. When it returns, it will need our full essence. That's the beautiful thing about this philosophy that I'm processing right now. You don't have to work hard. There is no effort. You don't have to run to catch up with it. It is catching up with you."

He hopped down from the rock.

"Also, somebody very wise once told me, 'You can either wait for the *pachacuti*, or you can *be* the *pachacuti*.' So choose now."

"I want to be part of the solution," I told Amado, "not part of the problem."

Amado turned his face up at me with a surprised look.

"You are not *part* of the solution, Princesa. You *are* the solution." And then, shrugging, "And perhaps there was no problem to begin with."

This stopped me in my tracks. *No problem to begin with.* Was this an example of *yanantin* consciousness in action? Amado seemingly held no blame for what I considered to be the deeply destructive impact of Western culture. Thinking back on the times we have spent together, I realize that Amado hardly ever seems to see the world as divided into problem versus solution. Instead, it seems to be that whatever he is presented with, on some level he deals with as part of a higher process and design—what he often jokingly refers to as the "cosmic referential program."

"Everything that happens represents a process that had to happen and is in complete harmony with the cosmos," he later told me. "Nothing happens down here without the will from above. That is a law. So, if people in the North are sleeping, there's no reason why we should panic or have fear. While a few people are hurting our planet so much, even that has its own time."

As Amado and I drove back to Cuzco, I thought of the Avenida del Sol mural, which displays so prominently the concept of time as returning to the point at which it began. Not exactly the same point, perhaps, but a new version thereof. Time may not be a set of fixed sequential relationships bound by cause and effect through which we must pass and can never return but a continuously repeating cycle or spiral. The seasons roll round and round. The rainy season becomes the dry season. The sun rises and sets and then rises again. The destroyer comes, but the Inca will rise again.

I thought about my own relationship to time, one informed by linear Western models.

Time, it felt, was not my friend. Time marched on, ever forward. Time deepened the lines in my face. It softened the regrets of the past but could never erase them. On some level, I felt trapped in time. I felt trapped by the fixed positions of present, past, and future. How often—in a therapy session, in an "enlightenment" seminar—had I been asked to review my past (for example, the events of my childhood) as something I must try to escape from or evolve out of in order for psychological healing to occur? According to so many Western psychological schools of thought, one's present difficulties have their roots in past traumas; therefore, it is believed that only by deconstructing our past and the remnants of it that we cling to can we achieve psychological health. Within this cause-and-effect mentality, we are trapped in the annals of our own personal history. The past is psychological quicksand from which we must try to escape and yet which holds us more strongly every time we tried to yank ourselves free. According to this perspective, I could deal with my past as productively as possible, but I could never escape it. And it was not just personal history that was apparently to blame, but the history of my family, of my culture, and of the entire human race. The Western linear model had developed an antagonistic relationship to the past and therefore could not seem to shake the unconscious dread of its contamination of the future. Certainly, this is an oversimplification in many ways. After all, deconstructing past events allows us to see how we relate to our present. And, yet, I couldn't help but think that in many cases we identify so heavily with our past that we cannot free ourselves from it.

Classen (1993) noted that "on a microcosmic level a *pachacuti* can take place within the body of an individual" (p. 33). So, too, does it occur within the *psyche* of each individual. Just as the world continually renews itself over the course of history, within an individual life one must pass through a series of personal *pachas* and *pachacutis*, when what is familiar and known does battle to retain dominance over the psyche in the face of what is unfamiliar and unknown. "Human nature is cyclical because it encompasses contradictory states of being," wrote Sullivan (1988, p. 627). Personal *pachacutis* tear apart our previously held beliefs, transforming us from one thing into another. A world asleep becomes a world awakened. Asleep. Awake. In these moments between, we do indeed feel as though we are being turned inside out. But through this process, something new is born. Perhaps even something like the evolved consciousness that Amado had spoken about.

In "looking for *yanantin*," I was consciously putting myself into a position for a personal *pachacuti* to take place. Was this why Amado and Juan Luis felt it was so important for me to join them in ceremony? As Allen (1998) noted, "Through ritualized exchange, opposed but complementary categories are drawn into conjunction . . . and categorical distinctions are blurred. . . . Andean ritual happens at an interface; it propels different dimensions of the cosmos into contact with one another and temporarily merges them" (pp. 148–149). Lévi-Strauss (1963) observed that mythological time (the form of time observed during ritual) is both reversible and nonreversible (p. 211). One can go forward or backward. Likewise, Sullivan (1988) wrote, "For all their distinctiveness, periodic time and mythic time may be linked through the ritual symbolism that reenacts the beginnings, the time before time lines and cycles definitively separated from one another" (p. 626). In ritual, theoretically at least, one is able to access multiple spaces and multiple times. Divisions of past, present, and future; locality; and causality cease to exist and therefore cease to create the blockages that Amado spoke of. In this way, healing takes place.

"The Medicine [San Pedro] allows the expression of that liberation in any moment," don Ignacio told me during ceremony one night. "Fears, pains, discomforts, feelings of guilt or inner or outer limitations of this life or past lives—the Medicine makes it manifest. That's the time that we will take advantage of, to help you liberate it fully. . . . There is no psychologist or psychiatrist, there's no clinical practice that can access the infinite dimensions of life that the Medicine can."

Later, Juan Luis explained it to me this way: "Every time you meet with yourself, with your essence, is a *pachacuti*. In life there is a process of rescuing yourself, or an important part of yourself, which you keep losing or, rather, missing. When you are with the Medicine, you reconnect to the part that you are missing. The Medicine initiates a *pachacuti*, which is a reencounter with yourself."

History is a line with no going backward, only forward, my Spanish teacher's brother had told me. *But in a spiral you can go forward and backward. It repeats. It renews. It is reversible. Within that spiral you can renew yourself. You can renew the world. Infinitely.*

Amado and I arrived back in town.

"Okay," I told him, "I'm convinced. I want to know *yanantin* better. I want to *be yanantin*. Like you said. Through ceremony."

Amado smiled and nodded.

"Good," he said. "We'll meet you in the plaza in two nights. Bring a sleeping bag."

FIGURE 6: © Carl A. Hyatt, 2000, Shaman at Ausangate

CHAPTER FOUR

Between Self and Other

D URING THAT FIRST FIELDWORK TRIP, I took a couple of Quechua lessons with a young Peruvian woman named Veronica. I liked Veronica a lot. She was bright and spunky and loved to tell stories. She would tell them to me in Spanish, though she confessed that she preferred speaking in Quechua, as it was much more expressive. "Like poetry," she said. Quechua, Veronica explained, has so many nuanced words for which Spanish and English have no exact equivalent that it is hard to achieve the same meaning, either in tone or in content.[1] The word *yanantin* is like that, she told me, when I asked her about it. The closest word in Spanish is *pareja*, meaning *pair*. But that is too superficial, she said. It does not encompass the whole idea of *yanantin*.

Although Veronica grew up in the rural highlands and was therefore surrounded by many Quechua-speaking people, when she was a child her parents forbade her to speak Quechua to her friends.

"But I did anyway," she told me, looking very pleased with herself. She then launched into another story about how on the mornings of certain Catholic ceremonies her father would lock the door and beat her brothers and sisters on the back of the legs with a whip as penance. After a few years of this, she began sneaking out through the window in her bedroom. She told the story with much humor and pride. I didn't learn much Quechua during our time together, but it was fun all the same, and I actually did learn a few things that helped me to understand certain aspects of *yanantin*.

During one lesson, I asked Veronica about the Quechua term *tinkuy*. Scholars (Allen, 1988, 2002; Bastien, 1978; Harrison, 1989; Joralemon & Sharon, 1993; Platt, 1986; Stone-Miller, 2002; Urton, 1981; Wilcox, 1999) have pointed to *tinkuy* as being an essential term in the Andean metaphysical outlook. When translated into English, the word *tinkuy* is usually said to refer to "the place where two rivers meet" (Allen, 1988; Harrison, 1989; Joralemon & Sharon, 1993). Some scholars also translate it as the "encountering or meeting of persons" and/or the "meeting of opposite forces" (Bastien, 1992, p. 159).

Amado disagreed with these more common definitions, stating emphatically, "*Tinkuy* is not the meeting. *Tinkuy* instead means the active part *after* the meeting. What do you do after the meeting? What happens? That is *tinkuy*, whether it is dance, whether it is war . . . anything. *Tinkuy* at this point is like, 'Okay, we've met. How do I allow myself deeper into you? What can I do for you so that you will never forget me?'"

Similarly, Harrison (1989) pointed to the active component of *tinkuy*: "The emphatic mention of *tinkuy* in daily conversation attests to its value as one of the primary categories for Andean society. It is a domain where two contrary or opposing forces or concepts coexist and intermingle" (p. 103). Cruz (2007) added,

> For the Andean man, the world is a dialectical process. Everything that exists in nature is made up of two opposite, contradictory, but at the end of the day, *complementary* forces. . . . In that dual thinking, that conception of duality, we see also complementarity, because the opposites as in the *tinkuy* get together to form unity. To create unity. And that is precisely what the *tinkuy* concept is talking about. When you have a partner or lovers, when they come together they are doing the *tinkuy*. They are uniting the two opposites, man and woman. Each has its own specific characteristics but when they come together they create the *tinkuy*, the unity. (n.p.)

Generally speaking, *tinkuy* is seen as the coming together of two oppos-ing but equal energies in order for a *yanantin* relationship to take place. The mixing of ingredients in medicine or cooking is sometimes referred to as *tinkuy* (Allen, 2002, p. 177). In the highland Andes, *solteros* (single people) from each of the rural villages meet on the pass once a year at Carnivale. There they dance and flirt in order to establish partnerships. This, too, is referred to as *tinkuy*.

My anthropologist friend, Jules, who works closely with the Q'ero peo-ple of the highland Andes, tells of how important this rite is to a world-view in which it is believed that things are lost without their complement. Jules told me stories of the reactions she received from the Q'ero when she revealed that she has no husband or partner. "For them, everything is dynamic, everything is complementary," she said. "That's why they are shocked when I say, 'No, I live alone, I don't have a *pareja*.'"

No matter what its context, the *tinkuy* encounter is a means by which opposing forces enter into a mutual recognition and mutual exchange of energies to establish (or reestablish) their connection as complementary forces. Platt (1986) pointed out that, in a *yanantin* relationship, "The ele-ments to be paired must first be 'pared' to achieve the 'perfect fit.' Here the crucial notion is that of the *sharing of boundaries* in order to create a har-monious coexistence" (p. 251). Through this coming together of opposing energies, there is an exchange of *ayni*, a reciprocal engagement through which the two become "pared." It is for this reason that among the indig-enous Andeans *ayni* is considered to be the balancing principle of Creation, for it is only through this kind of mutual exchange that opposing energies entering into this *tinkuy* become interdependent and therefore *yanantin* (Allen, 1988, 2002; Fernandez & Gutierrez, 1996; Heckman, 2003; Howard-Malverde, 1997; Zuidema, 1992).[2]

However, the Andean model of reality is by no means a utopian vision in which these oppositions are always easily and/or peacefully brought into a harmonious *yanantin* relationship. On the contrary, the "paring" of opposing forces can be violent as well as peaceful, depending on the con-text. In certain areas of the Andes, yearly *tinkuy* battles take place in which two groups (often groups of men but sometimes groups of women) meet and engage in physical combat. During one of our sessions, Veronica told me a story about sneaking into one of these villages to watch these bloody battles. She described witnessing a young man being knocked unconscious by a blow to the head. Moments later, he hopped up with a bleeding gash in his skull and ran off to brutalize someone else. Veronica hid behind a rock to watch, afraid that she might be seen. Had she been spotted, she said, she too would have been fair game for the rite.

"Horrible," she told me. "But very exciting."

These violent *tinkuy* battles have been described as the physical, ritual-ized enactment of the collision of opposing forces taking place within the cosmos. While bloody and even sometimes deadly, they are said to pro-mote fertility, moral equilibrium, and the resolution of boundary disputes (Allen, 1988, 2002; Bastien, 1992; Harrison, 1989). Bastien (1989) described the *tinkuy* battles as "a way of uniting opposite sides in a dialectic that clearly defines and recognizes the other as well as establishes their inter-dependence" (p. 76). Thus, while violent, the battles are seen as a means by which points of tension are released and harmony can be achieved, for as Allen (2002) suggested, "Rivals in battle, like lovers, are *yanantin* (a matched pair; helpmates). . . . Any release of energy—whether construc-tive or destructive—calls for collaboration" (p. 160).

In addition, Allen (2002) noted,

> In the *tinku*[3] battle, antagonists meet in a violent union. . . . [It is] simultaneously a dance, a fight, and a love affair . . . simultane-ously constructive and destructive. . . . Seen in this light, hostil-ity and violence are neither unequivocally negative nor ultimately destructive. . . . In both violent and peaceful modes, *tinkuy* signi-fies a mixture of different elements that brings something new to existence. (pp. 176–178)

When I asked Juan Luis about the *tinkuy* battles, he had a similar per-spective, regarding them as an opportunity for community healing. "This is the time in the year when all of them can solve their problems and their anger and all of it can come out in a fight," he told me. "They don't just say, 'Okay, there is a way of resolving this that can be peaceful so don't worry, just swallow your anger.' They prepare a whole year ahead of time for the moment that they will be able to bring all this anger out. It's one way of moving the *hucha* out of the system, out of the community."

As already noted, moving *hucha* out of a system—whether that is the physical or the mental system of the individual, an energetic exchange

between people, or within a community of interrelated beings as a whole—
is one of the primary tasks of Andean healing rites. According to Joralemon
and Sharon (1993), some Andean healers describe their ritual work—the
purpose of which is to harmonize the energies of a system (and, in doing
so, return it to a state of health and wholeness)—as engaging in a *tinkuy*
battle between heavy and light energies. In this encounter of energies, a
tension is created. While challenging, this tension is not, philosophically
speaking, considered a negative thing; rather, it is an essential aspect of
healing, for this tension is a source of energy through which balance is
created and/or restored.

For example, the primary healing tool of many Andean shamans is the
mesa, a cloth altar upon which the healer places a variety of sacred, healing
objects.[4] The *mesa* is said to act as a kind of energetic "map" that the healer
uses to perform his or her transformative work (Joralemon & Sharon, 1993;
Magee, 2002; Wilcox, 1999). Viewed as a microcosmic version of the greater
universe, the *mesa* allows the shaman to travel into the chaos of unbalanced
energies and, through various prayers and manipulations of sacred objects,
restore order and bring healing to those who require it.

Most *mesas* are split up into three major "fields."[5] The far left side of the
mesa is called "Campo Ganadero," "Field of the Magician." Other names
for the left side include "Field of Personal Gain," "Field of Domination," and
"Field of the Sly Dealer" (Joralemon & Sharon, 1993; Magee, 2002; Wilcox,
1999). The left side often contains objects that are believed to have "negative"
and/or aggressive characteristics that the healer must "tame" (Joralemon
& Sharon, 1993, p. 169). The energy of this section of the *mesa* is vital to the
healer's spiritual success, for here he or she gains the power to neutralize
acts of manipulation that may be harming his or her client and return the
negativity back to the sender. Work done in this area of the *mesa* helps the
healer release *hucha* from the patient (Wilcox, 1999). However, too much
emphasis on this side of the *mesa* leads one to rely too heavily on personal
will, leading to the temptation to exert one's power over other people, a
practice known as "sorcery" (Wilcox, 1999).

The far right side of the *mesa* is called "Campo Justiciero" or "Field
of Justice." It is also sometimes referred to as "Field of the Divine," "Field
of Divine Justice," "Curing Bank," and "Heavenly Bank" (Joralemon &
Sharon, 1993; Magee, 2002; Wilcox, 1999). This section is associated with
sami energy and is said to be the place where things are brought into

alignment according to the will of Spirit. Working in this field, the healer abandons personal agenda and allows the spirit world to take control of the situation. An individual who focuses too much on this side of the *mesa* may have trouble fulfilling his or her responsibilities of daily living. In addition, energetic actions may have trouble coming to fruition within the physical world (Wilcox, 1999).

Joralemon and Sharon (1993) reported that the *mesa* ritual

> represents the struggle between life-taking and life-giving forces, between left and right. But this struggle, this opposition, becomes a resolution by the shaman's re-affirmation of mastery over *both* the left and the right. . . . [The mesa] is a balancing act performed by an individual who stands above the contest by mastering both sides. It is thus that struggle—opposition—becomes passage, and cures are accomplished.[6] (p. 167)

As noted, the task of the Andean shaman is to harness both sides of the *mesa* and bring their complementary energies into harmony (Glass-Coffin, 2004; Joralemon & Sharon, 1993; Magee, 2002; Wilcox, 1999). This *tinkuy* between the two sides takes place in the center of the *mesa*, in the "Campo Medio" or "Field of the Middle." The healer who has learned to bring the two sides of the *mesa* into complementarity is called a *seguro* (meaning *sure* or *certain*), indicating that he or she has reached a state of physical, mental, emotional, and spiritual safety and can competently harness the two sides of the *mesa*, thus creating a dynamic interaction between light and heavy energies through which the healer can resolve the conflicts in the patients' lives that are creating illness (Joralemon & Sharon, 1993; Magee, 2002; Wilcox, 1999).

In a similar way, it seems that the *tinkuy* battles of the highland Andes represent a process in which opposing energies are identified, brought into conflict, mediated, and then transformed into complementary terms through a reciprocal exchange of energies and power. It is a means by which mutual recognition is achieved, in which similarities as well as differences are identified, for as Allen (2002) pointed out, "If there were no basic similarity between the combatants, they could not join in battle; but if there were no differences between them, they would not have a reason to fight" (p. 177).

Although somewhat horrified by the thought of it, as I reflected on these ideas, it was—at least in theory—somewhat possible for me to understand the positive aspects of the *tinkuy* battles performed in this ritualized context. At the beginning of my graduate schoolwork, I had become enchanted by the eighteenth-century philosopher G. W. F. Hegel's (1804/1977) story of "The Master and the Slave." As an allegory, "The Master and the Slave" reflects how seemingly hostile encounters can be understood as creative, positive, and even essential to our own development as human beings.

The story goes something like this: In the beginning, a consciousness emerges. At first it is alone—a singular, undifferentiated entity. While this condition is fine for a while, because it is alone it cannot become self-aware, for consciousness must interact with another consciousnesses if it is to develop *self*-consciousness. *I can only be me if there is someone or something else that is not me to compare myself to.* In order to become self-aware, one needs a mirror. One needs someone or something separate from the self to reflect one's identity as an individual.

The original consciousness yearns to know itself, to become self-aware. Eventually, another self-consciousness emerges. The two consciousnesses enter into what could be viewed as a kind of *tinkuy*. But while the initial encounter fulfills each one's yearning for a nonself "other" through which it can achieve self-awareness, each consciousness eventually feels threatened by the existence of its opposite, believing it to be a threat to its sense of control over the world. In dealing with this fear, each demands recognition of its superiority over the other. A love-hate dynamic results, one that is equal parts attraction and repulsion, for while each needs the other in order to attain self-awareness, there is an equal and opposing dread of the other's existence. To resolve this tension (both the inner tension that each feels and also the tension between them), the two consciousnesses engage in a battle for dominance.

Eventually, one consciousness overcomes the other and forces it to bend to its will. Rather than risk annihilation at the hands of this stronger presence, the defeated consciousness becomes the "Slave" and the victor the "Master." The Slave is put to work creating the world according to the Master's bidding. The Master goes about his life within a world that the Slave has made. This arrangement seems like a positive thing to the Master, who has now achieved control over everything around him or her. But to possess or destroy something means to rob it of its individuality, of its contrast to the self, of its "otherness." Over time, an interesting shift occurs (though typically so slowly that neither consciousness is aware of it at first). Despite the fact that the world that the Slave has created is of his Master's bidding, the sweat that created it is the Slave's own, making the world a reflection of him or her. Realizing this, the Slave earns self-respect and identity. At the same time that this occurs, the Master starts to *lose* self-identity, for not only is the world no longer a reflection of him or her, but by subjugating his or her opposite, the Slave is no longer a viable counterpart against which the Master can come to know himself or herself. As this shift in identity occurs, the two of them eventually trade positions: The Slave becomes the Master and the Master now the Slave. And so it goes, on and on. Hegel believed that the two would continue this flip-flopping back and forth until a time came that both consciousnesses recognized their interdependence and necessity to one another's existence.

It was in this light that I began to consider the features of the self-other relationships found within the Andean model of reality and, in particular, regarding the *tinkuy* battles.[7] While horrifying in many respects, I could also see how any encounter—whether violent or peaceful—is a form of communication through which two energies can come to know each other and know themselves and therefore achieve some kind of intimacy. After all, intimacy includes hostility at times, doesn't it? Through these encounters, in which the violence is put within a ritualized framework and is thus intentional and contextual, points of similarity and difference can be identified and the buildup of *hucha* resolved. In doing so, the two energies can become "pared" into a *yanantin* relationship. The two opposing forces become collaborators in conflict in order to achieve complementarity.

While the yearly battles are one extreme example of this confluence of opposing energies, Amado pointed out that the same kind of *tinkuy* encounters—both violent and peaceful—occur every day within the context of our interpersonal relationships. When I pressed him to explain this idea further, he described a three-stage process through which energies typically engage in a harmonization process, commenting on what happens when we are not conscious of this progression. The stages, he said, are *tupay*, *tinkuy*, and *taqe*. The progression, as explained by Amado, is as follows:

"*Tupay* is the meeting point in a relationship. Whenever you meet a person, whenever you meet an *apu* or whatever energy, *tupay* is that encounter. It is very sacred. It is very powerful. In partnership, in wife to husband relationship, *tupay* is very, very powerful. There are ceremonies each year that are specifically celebrated for *tupay*, for having this encounter. Nowadays, a lot of people get married during this first level of meeting. A lot of people say, 'Oh, wow, it is so powerful, it is so strong.' And they go for that relationship right away.

"Then the next level is *tinkuy*. *Tinkuy* is a battle. It is challenging each other—who knows more, who is the stronger, who is smartest, who is in control. All of that starts coming out. These are all the other parts that you are to know about your soul mate or partner. When the love is strong, then some people will get married in *tinkuy*. That's powerful. The people who get married in *tupay*, often they will discover that there were all these other levels that they had to go through. That is why there are a lot of divorces, because they did not arrive to the *tinkuy* in order to find their balance. So, when they arrive at *tinkuy*, a lot of couples divorce or separate. But if the love is strong and they have arrived at *tinkuy*, then they will get married.

"Only by going through this *tinkuy* level, which is going through all those challenges and all those problems and all those battles and difficulties, can you arrive at *taqe*. *Taqe* represents that cosmic force in which the two become one. That other partner, that soul mate, not only is the complement, but she becomes the very foundation of my being. I cannot do anything without her support or her company or her energy or her strength. And, of course, that doesn't go one way. That level of *taqe* becomes the finest energy that can bring transformation and change to the world. If you have children in that third level, in *taqe*, you can be almost sure that these children will become very powerful leaders. *Very* powerful leaders. For a lot of the people, it would be very delicate to have children when they are in the *tinkuy* [stage]. And even more when you are just in *tupay*. But, nevertheless, there has to be *tupay* for there to be *tinkuy*, and there has to be *tinkuy* for there to be *taqe*.

"In the communities, from the moment teenage people meet, they are already acknowledging these three stages. [We have known] since the Incan times that a relationship isn't just an accident; neither is it something you can just take for granted. Rather, it is the most delicate flower to take care of, from the moment of its seeding, to the moment of its blooming, to the moment when it's going to go into an offering, into the fire."

Amado added that when speaking of this idea, it is important to point out that in the Andes this necessity of achieving harmonious relationships is not limited to encounters between human beings but includes the bonds and liaisons between all entities—animate and inanimate, tangible and intangible, seen and unseen. The indigenous Andean model of reality is one of animism, the belief that all things that exist are in some sense alive and conscious and that it is not just possible *but absolutely necessary* to engage in reciprocal relationships with all beings of the cosmos.

As Vasquez (1998) wrote,

> [In the Andes] everything is alive and important; nothing is inert and nothing is superfluous. The very stone is alive, it speaks and the peasant converses with it as person to person. It is not that the peasant extends the notion of person to the stone (which is generally understood as "personification") but rather that, for the peasant, the stone is alive . . . In the Andean context we cannot speak either of the inanimate as opposed to the animate, or of the essential as opposed to the contingent. (p. 97)

Vasquez's (1998) statement about "animate" and "inanimate" being abstractions is an interesting one and so unlike the sharp dividing line between the world of the living and the world of the nonliving created by Western philosophical models.

In discussing this idea, Amado said to me, "You know how that philosopher used to say, 'I think therefore I am'?"

"Descartes? Sure," I said.

"We think it is the craziest thing to say! 'I think therefore I am' . . . ¡por favor! We'd say, 'I am first, and then I think it over!' I mean, I can't even take for granted who I am, only *that* I am, first and foremost. We play with that. We think it over."

In his study of lunar cosmology and astronomy in Misminay, Peru, Urton (1981) described the cycles of the moon as being divided into the phases of *wañu, cuscan,* and *pura*. In explaining these stages, Urton suggested that the Quechua term *wañu* translates most directly into English as *inanimate* or *lifeless*. Its complement, *pura*, "stands at the other end representing animate *in relation* to varying degrees of inanimate" (p. 84).[8] Urton wrote, "As a classifier, pura groups together all members of a class or sequence which are in a *relationship of interaction*" [emphasis in original text] (p. 84).

Urton's (1981) mention of the distinction between these words presents us with another opportunity to consider the places where a translation between Quechua and English fails us—epistemologically, ontologically, and otherwise. It also points to a significant feature in how Andean philosophical models relate to self-other interactions. Here, too, language affects our relationship to the world, not only in content but perhaps just as much so in style. Veronica had told me that the Quechua language is like poetry. Given this, it made sense to me that the Quechua-speaking people have such a deep sense of connection to and intimacy with the world around them, for as Nin (1968) wrote, "The poet brings the dissected [world] to life, because the poet is primarily *the lover of the world*, and therefore he alone can make us fall in love. Very few of us are necrophilic and fall in love with dead matter after it has been dissected by the intellectual" (p. 98).

As mentioned earlier, as my research developed, I came to realize that the *relationship* between entities or energies is perhaps *the* essential component when gaining an understanding of the nature of complementary opposition in Andean philosophical models. In Andean thought, the relationship between entities or energies is considered an ever-changing condition, one that is constantly shifting, creating, and recreating itself with each encounter. Because of this, the achievement of "balance" is never a static condition but is always context-dependent and requires continual maintenance according to each circumstance. Self-other encounters are therefore never taken for granted but reassessed with every situation. There is an acknowledgement that self and other are never and can never be separated, for each depends on the other for mutual recognition and reciprocity.

During the opening ceremonies of The Heart of the Healer (THOTH) conference held in Pisaq, Peru, in July 2007, a shaman from the Andean highlands spoke of *tinkuy* as "the place where opposites meet and where our differences become our strengths." I was intrigued by this statement. The next day, anthropologist Bonnie Glass-Coffin, an expert on Andean *curanderismo*, spoke at length about Andean philosophical models. She used the term *tinkuy* often in her talk, referring to it as a means by which we can achieve connection to one another and to the rest of the world, acknowledging that it is in fact through pain and loss that new life grows.

By consciously engaging in *tinkuy* encounters, Glass-Coffin said, we can achieve balance and healing.

After her talk, I asked Glass-Coffin if she could speak more about the idea of *tinkuy* as a state in which "our differences become our strengths."

"How as individuals do we become conscious of our differences and the strengths that lie within them through *tinkuy*?" I asked her.

Her response was this: "It is a beautiful question, and I think, for me, that this has been one of the greatest teachings I've received . . . What I've learned is this: When faced with the challenge of someone who has a point of view different from our own, or a tradition different from our own, I feel that our tendency is to move to a place of what we call in anthropology 'ethnocentrism,' by which I mean that we tend to interpret our world from a point of view where we are in the center, and what we do from that center is all that is normal and right and everything else out there is somehow weird and different. And when we begin to be able to embrace rather than judge, to suspend disbelief, as they say in film, rather than try and interpret everything from our own life experience, when we truly open ourselves to engaging with the rest of the world in a way that we are willing to surrender our control over knowing that what we know is right and good, when we are willing to surrender to the fact that we don't know, then I think that's where that place of *tinkuy*—an encounter of coming together in love rather than judgment—can really begin."

"The thing with *tinkuy*," she continued, "at least in the Andes, which is of course where the word comes from, is these encounters are not peaceful, quiet, calm encounters. The term *tinkuy* comes when two massive rivers flow together, and if you have ever seen two rivers coming together during flood season, the result is not quiet. And so, to apply this concept of *tinkuy* to a discussion of differences as strengths, we need to be able to be accepting of every piece of the chaos that is moved within ourselves. We need to be able to accept and be accepting of those feelings of judgment that we carry. We need to be able to move from a place of judgment for its own sake to a place of honoring and then releasing our judgment, our ego, our fear. We need to acknowledge that in each of us we are ego *and* inspiration and that those two are divine in and of themselves. Rather than trying to split off and say, 'Well, this is ego, this isn't divinely inspired and so therefore I'm not going to listen to this half,' we move to a place of being willing to accept and embrace [both]. Where it all starts from, at least for me, is that sense of being willing to let go and surrender that sense of control that we know who we are or that we know anything in the world. That's why I would say that *tinkuy* is so good. There is a lesson to be learned from it all if we are willing to be open to the lesson that every *tinkuy* that comes across our path is a lesson that we can learn from."

Her statement resonated with me deeply, for during my first San Pedro ceremony with Amado and Juan Luis, I found myself engaged in a kind of *tinkuy* battle. It was a battle that unfolded within my own consciousness and most definitely forced me to surrender control over my own mind and its habitual need for control. Allen (2002) described *tinkuys* as "powerful, dangerous places full of liberated and uncontrollable forces" (p. 176). Indeed, during my first San Pedro ceremony, two conflicting thoughts met and engaged in a battle for dominance—one that felt as though it might tear my mind apart. But it didn't. What resulted instead was a kind of synthesis—not one in which the two thoughts negated each other and dissolved into one but one in which the tension created by the encounter caused each to become strengthened in and of itself. Strangely, this allowed the two to coexist side by side, like poles in a magnetic field. This, I would come to understand, was the essence of *yanantin*.

FIGURE 7: © Carl A. Hyatt, 2004, Cuzco at Night

CHAPTER FIVE

Chaupin

ON FRIDAY EVENING, I arrived at the plaza early to rent a sleeping bag and an inflatable mat from one of the tourist centers lining the square. I felt a slight nervousness wondering what the evening would hold, although now that I had made up my mind to do it, my nervousness was more excitement than fear.

The mind is a funny thing, isn't it?

I eventually spotted Amado's car and jogged across the street to meet him and Juan Luis. Amado's cousin, Marco, was sitting in the driver's seat, with Juan Luis riding shotgun. Amado sat in the back. I barely recognized them at first. All three of them were dressed in traditional ceremonial costume—brightly colored ponchos and the warm, woven *chullo* hats of the highland Andes. As their heads swung round to greet me, the pompoms hanging down from their *chullos* swung in unison.

"*Buenas tardes*, Princesa," they called out. Juan Luis got out of the car and helped me put my things into the back. I climbed in next to Amado and the four of us zoomed up the mountain and out of town. Soon we were out of the city and driving through the farmlands of the valley just below

Cuzco. The landscape was lush and emerald green from all the rain of the past several months. In some areas, the ground had been cut open through tilling, exposing luscious blood-red soil beneath. All the colors of the land glowed against the darkening sky. We listened to a kind of Nuevo-Andean *zampoña* music as we drove—traditional flute music flavored with a more modern, electric touch. It was a strange juxtaposition of old and new, and I liked it. Everything in that moment seemed heightened, including my own joy.

I turned to Amado, who met the glow in my eyes with a smile and a hug. As we embraced, I said, "Amadocito, I don't know how this happened, but I am so glad I'm here."

"And I am glad you are here, too, my sister from the North," he said, patting my hand.

Later on the drive, I asked Amado, "Will the San Pedro make me sick like *ayahuasca*?" (A powerful hallucinogenic preparation used in the Peruvian rain forest, *ayahuasca* is often accompanied by a violent purging process in which anything that isn't part of one's basic anatomy comes rushing out in *mass exodus*—from both ends.)

"No, Princesa. Juan Luis's preparation is gentle. You might feel the urge to throw up at first, but that urge will pass if you let it."

He handed me a bottle of water and instructed me to drink it. Once the ceremony began, we would not be ingesting anything other than the San Pedro, and it was important not to get dehydrated.

Half an hour after leaving Cuzco, we reached the town of Chincheros, where Amado grew up and where much of his family still lived. It was completely dark now, and the town's narrow road was illuminated only by the golden fluorescent glow coming from a small store tucked into a row of squat adobe buildings that lined the street. We pulled up across from it and Amado and Marco got out and ran off on some errand.

As we waited, Juan Luis and I chatted. I asked him about his life, and he told me that he was currently living in the home of his teacher and mentor don Ignacio, from whom he learned to work with San Pedro. He had married don Ignacio's daughter, Claudia. The two of them had a little boy.

I asked Juan Luis about his work with San Pedro, how he started on the path of these medicine teachings.

"I started on this path when I was a child," he told me. "I dreamed a lot. I used to hang out with my older brothers. I used to go to the jungle a lot.

And when I got home I would tell my mother about riding with my friends on the elephants. My mother said I shouldn't lie. But I would swear that we had ridden on the elephants. I used to fly a lot. I do not think it was all childish magic. Later, when I had finished high school, I started to study under a [shamanic] teacher in Lima. I started to appreciate my essence and my love of the unknown. I loved what I learned about what I was—my essence, my Andean roots. My teacher taught me a lot about who I was. He told me to look at myself. I felt part of something. I was not aware of what it was, but I was already part of something. And step by step, I started to walk.

"Later, I had the chance to travel a little around the North, which is the home of San Pedro. I did not have too much experience [with San Pedro], but I did know of the Medicine and I was very scared of it. Sometimes someone is afraid of what they don't know. But life led me to know San Pedro, and through it I learned to see the *huacas*, the sacred places. I was not afraid anymore. I was feeling a lot of peace. Later, when I came back to live in Cuzco, I got a job. I returned to college. I met my wife and her father, the healer don Ignacio. I learned from him and added my new knowledge to the knowledge that I had obtained in the North. I wanted to know more. My heart called me and I started to walk with him. I followed him constantly. I learned a lot from him and everything that surrounded him. And through him I met other teachers.

"Now it is my life. I have been working with San Pedro for eight years. Only two years ago after a long preparation did I have permission [from my teacher] to give the Medicine to other people. When I am in ceremony, the Medicine flows with me. What is acting through me is not me, it is the Medicine. I am only a manifestation, a channel."

Marco and Amado appeared out of the darkness carrying four large bottles of beer and an armload of firewood, all of which they piled in the back of the car. We continued up the mountain, winding our way around the hairpin turns. I felt grateful for the darkness, which kept me blissfully ignorant of the steep drop that undoubtedly lay below us. Eventually, Marco pulled off onto a flat area next to the road. We all jumped out, grabbed our gear, and headed toward a fire pit about 50 feet away. At 13,000 feet above sea level, it was cold up there. Really, really cold. Several years earlier, while trekking in the Andes, I had spent a night on top of a glacier at an altitude of about 16,000 feet. At that height, cold is no longer cold. It was the kind of cold that has gone beyond itself, a cold so cold that one's body can barely register it—kind of like when a person gets an ice cube stuck to his or her finger. Here on the mountain in Chincheros, however, the frigid air sunk deep into one's bones without that strangely comforting—though often deadly—numbness. At first, I thought it was just me, that I was simply not used to these temperatures, but then I heard Juan Luis make a joke about this mountain being the "freezer of Cuzco."

Amado and Juan Luis set about building a fire, which, once going, took the edge off the bone-piercing chill. I wrapped my sleeping bag around me and sat down by the fire, watching and waiting. The wood must have been damp, for it crackled and steamed as it burned, spitting streams of thick smoke. Between the smoke and the thin air, my lungs had to strain to get enough oxygen, and I felt as though someone was sitting on my chest.

Marco saw my discomfort. "Don't fight it," he told me. "Just try to breathe through it."

Eventually, the three men gathered around the fire and motioned to me to stand up. Juan Luis pulled a large plastic container out of his bag and poured some of the thick liquid into a silver cup. Whispering soft prayers under his breath, he held the cup up to the sky, then to the earth, and then poured several drops onto the ground. *Pachamama always drinks first.* He brought the cup to his lips and drank the contents of the cup down without stopping. Amado poured *agua florida* onto Juan Luis's palms. Juan Luis rubbed his hands together, clapped three times, then brought them up to his nose and inhaled deeply three times. He poured another cup of the San Pedro and handed it to Amado, who then repeated the same process.

The third cup was for me. I shivered a little as Juan Luis put it in my hands. The two of us held the cup together for a few moments as Juan Luis spoke the traditional prayers:

"Pachacamac, Wiracochan, Inti Texymuyuc, Qaylla, Pachayachacheq, Tunupa Usapa, Pachamama.

"Allintachaskiriway kaytukuysonqo.

"Invocando la divina presencia, del maestro Jesus, de todos los apus, de todos los aukis.

"De los seres divinales. Invocando la divina presencia, de los Canchisilla.

"Vengan, vengan, vengan aqui.

"Se manifiesten en nuestros corazones, en esta medicina sagrada, nos permitan entrar en sus mundos, en sus cuerpos, en sus mentes, en su ser."

("Pachacamac,[1] Wiracochan,[2] Inti Texymuyuc,[3] Qaylla,[4] Pachayachacheq,[5] Tunupa Usapa,[6] Pachamama.[7]

"Acknowledge our gifts that come with all our heart.

"Invoking the divine presence, Master Jesus, all the apus, all the aukis.

"The divine beings, the divine presence, the seven rays children of the
sun, the rainbow lineage.

"Come, come, come here.

"Manifest in our hearts, in the sacred Medicine.

"Permit us to enter in your worlds, in your body, in your mind, in your
being.")

Juan Luis stuck his thumb in the liquid and rubbed some of it onto my
forehead, saying, "*Que hace sea, que así es*" ("So be it, so it is").

Then he nodded at me. "Drink."

And so I drank. The taste was not as bad as I had imagined it would be.
It was bitter—yes, very bitter—but not terrible. He poured the perfume into
my hands and I did as they had done, wincing a little as the sharp alcohol
scent of the perfume stung my nasal cavities.

"Princesa," Amado said in a low voice behind me, "this is your
yanantin."

The four of us sat down around the fire. There were a few moments of
silence, and then Juan Luis began to speak.

"The purpose of this ceremony is healing," he told us. "In order to heal,
we must not attempt to destroy the heavy energy that we carry but to move
it through us."

He continued, "Heavy energy is a part of us. We have accepted it. These
heavy thoughts are our children. You have created them. Sometimes they
make you feel as if you are irritated and suffocating. Like the smoke from
this fire. You can't breathe. You always feel as if there is something else, that
you lack something. The hard part is to let this energy go. You know you
are healing yourself when you start to feel some freedom from that. When
you free this energy, you start to feel relief. You start to relax your spirit."

He paused for a moment, and then said, "This is very important. Not
long ago we used to work just like everybody does. We thought that you
had to destroy, that there was a need to cut. But with the Medicine we enter
into a higher level of consciousness. The Medicine tells us that there is no
need to destroy anything, because if you do, you are destroying yourself
because the energy that makes us heal and the energy that makes us suffer

are intelligent energies. They know our thoughts and they make us think and feel in order to feed themselves. They feed on our pain. They feed on our suffering. So, what we have to do is not to kill them, just as a father would not kill his own son. What a father wants for his son is that he be free, that he be pure. This is the mission that we have to achieve within ourselves. We have to get rid of that heavy energy and get in touch with that energy that makes us happy. We have to receive that energy. It teaches us a lot of wonderful things. That energy teaches us that we can learn from our mistakes. Through that energy we can transform ourselves. That is why alchemy exists. It's the teaching of transformation. And what are we to transform? We are to transform ourselves into beings of peace and beings of love."

"How do we do that?" I wanted to know.

Juan Luis nodded.

"It starts with forgiveness," he said. "The most important part of forgiveness is beginning a new life, and not looking back. It is leaving behind all that has happened. In order to forgive properly, we have to enter into forgiveness on three levels.

"The first level is to forgive oneself, because, having accepted the garbage that someone has thrown at us with bad intention, it is now our responsibility. Someone throws it who is envious, who is angry, and who has bad energy. This garbage doesn't penetrate but bounces off. Then we pick it up as our own. But that garbage doesn't belong to us, although we consider it ours. Therefore, the first level of forgiveness is to forgive ourselves for having accepted that garbage.

"The second level of forgiveness is to forgive generally. There are people who harm us. They do this consciously or unconsciously. A lot of people think they are doing us a favor, but they are not. So, we have to forgive those people.

"The third level of forgiveness is asking forgiveness for our own actions, because just like all those people who threw garbage at us, we also throw garbage. If we didn't, we wouldn't be here. That is why we come into this life—to clean our karma and to strengthen our dharma,[8] in order to close our circle of love here. On Pachamama we have the circle of our physical family, another circle of our spiritual family, and another one of our cosmic family. We have to carry out our mission and clean these circles. After we have cleaned them, we can transcend to another level. Forgiveness helps us to do that. It helps us to clean our situations, to clean our circle, to clean our relationships with other people, and mainly, our relationship with ourselves. If we are not at peace with ourselves, we will not be at peace with the world. So, the most important thing is to clean up our relationship with our self. That is why the first level of forgiveness is to forgive oneself."

"What happens after we do this?" I asked. "What happens when we are fully 'healed'?"

"Then we are ready for the teachings," he said.

"What teachings?" I asked.

"The Medicine teachings from the cosmos."

With that, I had to be satisfied. The four of us lay down in our sleeping bags and closed our eyes, waiting for the San Pedro to take effect.

Time passed. I must have fallen asleep, because I was suddenly jolted awake, feeling as though I had just remembered something important, something *essential* even—as if a thousand dreams that I had ever had but then forgotten had returned to me all at once. There was a brief moment of awareness, and then it was gone. Frustratingly gone.

And then, in the next moment, another sensation overcame me, one that can only be described as a simultaneous splitting and a joining of myself. While on the one hand I was aware of having a very strong sense of emotion—many emotions, in fact, perhaps even *all* emotions—another part of me felt completely detached, almost *clinical*. It was as though I could observe my emotions in a completely objective way while at the same time be fully subjectively saturated with feelings—ecstatic and painful and everything in between.

I heard a rustling as Juan Luis got out of his own sleeping bag and came over to me. Although I hadn't moved or made a sound, he had somehow known that I was awake. Later, when I asked him how he had known that I had begun the journey, he responded, "San Pedro opens up a connection that is usually unconscious. That connection is always there, but often we are not conscious of it."

He knelt down beside me and lowered his face to mine.

"What feelings are you having, Princesa? What thoughts?"

I struggled for words, partially for words in Spanish to explain what I was feeling but mostly for words in *any* language to try to describe the sensation.

Finally, I said, "I am happy and sad all at once. But I also feel nothing. Nothing at all. How can that be?"

Juan Luis nodded, as if pleased. "Good," he said. "That's good. There are no contradictions. This is the foundation. Everything is complementary. Being sad and being happy are states of mind. It's best to be in the middle. Not too hot, not too cold. You have to look for a balance point. It's like when they take your temperature. If you are in the middle, you are fine. Try not to feel too sad or too happy. Seek peace of mind."

He poured another cup of the San Pedro and handed it to me, nodding for me to drink. After doing so, I lay back in my sleeping bag, looking up at the colors of the moon. It was exquisite—light pinks and greens and golds all swirling together in a misty haze. How had I never seen that before? The sky itself was nothing less than miraculous—crystal clear, like a big dome placed over me. How amazing they were, those streaks of constellations. Had I ever seen so many stars at one time?

And then, as I watched, the stars began to move, to dance. I closed my eyes, expecting them to be still when I opened them, but even then they continued to hop around the sky like fireflies. I was overjoyed. I felt as though I had been let in on the deepest secret of the cosmos—that the stars move when no one is watching them.

And yet, at the same time that I watched them dance, seeing this unfold with my eyes wide open, there was a part of my mind that *knew* this was not real, that it was an illusion created by the San Pedro, that the stars do not really move. As much as I *wanted* them to move—as much as I wanted them to be conscious and alive and joyful—another part of me reminded myself that this could not be. But then I would look back up at them again and they *would* be moving anyway, despite the insistence of that logical voice. And then I would wonder again if maybe they really *do* move

don't move
do move
don't move
after all.

Which was real? Both seemed real, and while on the one hand I felt euphoric, at the same time I feared that my mind would split in two from the weight of the contradiction.

Moving or not moving?
Real or not real?

The tension created in my consciousness by these two opposing thoughts reached a kind of critical mass, a *tinkuy*, one that I thought might be too much to withstand. But then, suddenly, the two thoughts in their fight for dominance seemed to wear each other out. It was then that I understood.

It was *both*. *The stars both move and don't move*, all at once. In that moment, I accepted fully and completely the stars' movement and non-movement as equal realities, without question or doubt or the need to make it one or the other.

And then, another *Eureka!* moment.

For years, I had been trying to understand the quantum physics theory of "Schrödinger's Cat." Schrödinger's Cat is a thought experiment that is often used to illustrate how, at the subatomic level, the laws of Newtonian physics—which are based on principles of noncontradiction—cease to apply and paradoxes abound. Here, subatomic events both take place and do not take place all at once.

The theory of Schrödinger's Cat proposes a scenario in which a living cat is placed in a steel chamber containing a vial of poisonous acid and a small amount of radioactive substance. A device is set up so that if even a single atom of the radioactive substance decays, a hammer will break the vial of acid and kill the cat. Because the box is sealed, the person observing the experiment cannot know whether the vial has been broken. According to rules as they are said to apply at the quantum level, because we cannot know which outcome has occurred, there comes a point at which *the cat is both alive and dead*. This presents us with the question: When does a quantum system stop existing as a mixture of states and become one or the other? According to many quantum physicists, it is only after we as conscious observers open the box and look inside that the cat becomes either dead or alive. This situation is sometimes called "quantum indeterminacy" or the "observer's paradox."

This whole concept had never made sense to me on either a logical or an intuitive level. But now, staring up at the stars and witnessing their equal movement and nonmovement, I understood how such a thing could be.

Schrödinger's cat is dead!
Schrödinger's cat is not dead!
The stars move when no one is watching!
The stars do not move . . . ever!
Dead!
Not dead!
Moving!

Not moving!

That was it. *Yanantin.* Captured by this vision, life took on new significance for me. It became clear how much time and energy is wasted trying to determine what was true or untrue; whether we people are wonderful or terrible, splendid or savage; or, on a more personal level, whether I myself was lovable or entirely unlovable. These roles that we create for ourselves, the divine and the demonic . . . at what point do we stop existing as a mixture of both and become one thing or the other? It is when we are in the process of observing ourselves, of self-reflecting, of trying to figure out if we are one thing or the other and act accordingly.

I was thrilled. I had to tell someone, if only so that I wouldn't forget it. Amado was asleep, snoring, on the other side of the fire. I tried to explain it to Juan Luis, but in my excitement my Spanish got all jumbled up and all that came out was a nonsensical, "A cat! In a box! And a hammer! The cat is dead and not dead!" Although I could tell he was trying hard to take me seriously, Juan Luis burst out laughing. I began to laugh, too. Feeling ecstatic, I lay back and tried to get the stars to move again, but they didn't. The moment had passed, though the teaching still lingered.

Eventually, I fell asleep, and the next time I awoke it was morning. I sat up in my sleeping bag, pushing my hair out of my eyes and squinting in the sunlight. Because it had been dark when we arrived the night before, I hadn't seen anything past the ridge that we were camped on, and here in the morning light the sight took my breath away. Directly across from me were the snow-capped peaks of Apu Veronica, Apu Wakawillka, and Apu Chicón. Although miles away, they were such imposing features of the landscape that in that moment I had an understanding of a form of consciousness that acknowledged them not just as living entities but as lords and deities. It was hard not to just sit and stare at them, completely mesmerized by their existence.

Slowly, Amado, Juan Luis, and Marco began to emerge from inside their dew-soaked sleeping bags. The four of us gathered around the now-smoldering campfire. Amado pulled out a glass from his backpack and opened one of the bottles of beer. He passed it around, with each of us taking turns finishing off a glass and then passing it on to the next person. An hour later we had finished off all four bottles of beer.[9]

Standing around, waiting for my turn to drink, I combed my hair with my fingers and found my first white hair. I showed it to them.

"White hair is a sign of wisdom," Juan Luis said with a teasing smile.

"But there's only one!" I laughed.

"Yes," Amado said, "but it is a beginning."

At 8:00 a.m., we grabbed our things, cleaned up the campsite, and piled back into the car. We drove back to Chincheros, stopping at Amado's in-laws' house where we were met with a delicious, steaming meal of *choclo*, *chile relleño*, and *pollo al horno*. By 9:30, we were on our way back to Cuzco.

As they dropped me off in the plaza, I hugged and kissed each of them in turn. I gave Juan Luis an extra big hug and thanked him for his guidance the night before.

"It was beautiful," I said. "Perfect."

Holding me by the shoulders, Juan Luis looked deeply into my eyes and said, "Now you can have trust again. Not in me, not in Amado, but in yourself."

With that, the experience closed and the three of them drove off. I returned to the store where I had rented my sleeping bag and mat. The owner seemed unconcerned about my disheveled appearance and the dampness of the bag. Afterward, I hailed a cab and returned home. I was sad that this "perfect" moment was over and that the connection that I had felt—to myself, to the cosmos, to my three friends—felt so distant. During ritual, a link is established—between you and the other people in the ceremony, and between you and the cosmos. And when that is gone, there is a deep sense of loss, even loneliness. Only later I would realize that it was the same feeling of having spent all night with a lover and achieved an ecstasy that comes from great intimacy and communion with another person. When the lover leaves the next morning, there is a tragic emptiness.

I left Peru at the end of April and returned home with more than 100 pages of field notes and more questions than answers. Not long after I returned home, I was doing some reading of the literature on Andean cosmology, and I came across the Quechua word *chaupin* or *chawpi*.[10] Literally translated, *chaupin/chawpi* means the "middle region" or the "intermediate zone" (Platt, 1986, p. 232). It is described as a center point in which two things come together. It is, the literature seemed to imply, meant to indicate a place where the initial opposition of disparate elements is neutralized.

During a conversation I had with the noted Peruvian anthropologist Jorge Flores Ochoa, he suggested that in order for a *yanantin* relationship to occur, "There needs to be a *chawpi*, a middle, an intermediate unifier between the two. An axis. . . . It separates in order to unite. *Chawpi* is a medium. It is the interaction between the two."

The description of *chaupin/chawpi* is not unlike the descriptions given of the Hindu-Buddhist conception of *nirdvandva*, or what Watts (1969) described as "a state of consciousness to be found in the interval between two thoughts" (p. 197). Likewise, in his cartography of the psyche, Jung (1953/1956) wrote about the "midpoint" of the personality, "that ineffable something betwixt the opposites, or else that which unites them, or the result of conflict, or the product of energetic tension" (p. 242).

Was this what I had experienced staring at the stars that night? A reaching of this midpoint in which two thoughts came together and then finally resolved their tension by entering into a state in which both possibilities—the stars' movement and their nonmovement—could exist simultaneously? Perhaps so. While I can't say for sure what it was, the psychological effects of the experience were profound. In the days and months afterward, I found myself approaching the world and my own existence in a different way. Most notably was a lack of attachment to my own thoughts and judgments. Or to anyone else's, for that matter. Gone was the need to determine in every given moment what was "right" and what was "wrong." I noticed that during this time my interactions with people were easier, and I spent much less energy contemplating the minutia of my own existence. Whether the world was splendid or savage, or whether I was splendid or savage, did not really matter. These things now coexisted in a way that they could not before. And it felt great.

In discussing this experience and its effects with a colleague, he argued that this lack of attachment, lack of discrimination of what is "good" and what is "bad," would lead to a dangerous complacency. But I disagreed. On the contrary, it seemed to me that when we let go of our attachment to proving one thing over the other, we are suddenly freed and left with massive amounts of energy with which we can engage with the world in a very harmonious way. Choosing between the two becomes unnecessary—one just acts. One just is and then does. That, as Juan Luis said, is healing. It is ultimate psychological freedom.

After returning home from this first fieldwork trip, I came across a passage in my reading that reflected the experience I had in ceremony so exactly that it gave me epistemological chills:

The Andean does not experience her gazing at the rising of a particular constellation in a particular region on the horizon as a unidirectional act on her part. . . . Rather it is experienced as the constellation and gazer being united in a conversation. These conversations lead to wisdom rather than knowledge; wisdom emerges from the body-world interface; it is not an intellectual, conceptual, or symbolic "knowledge" or set of "beliefs" held in the mind. (Apffel-Marglin, 1998, p. 32)

Reading that, comparing it to my own experience, I suddenly under-stood what Amado had meant during that first meeting when he told me I needed to "download the information from the cosmos." Through an experience with San Pedro, I had become "united in conversation" with the cosmos, not metaphorically, but at a very literal level. In this way I had come to "know" *yanantin* in a way that I could integrate it—even just a little—and that changed my psychological sense of myself in a truly profound way.

FIGURE 8: © Carl A. Hyatt, 2006, Tenon Head, Chavín

CHAPTER SIX

The Lanzón

I RETURNED TO PERU the following September for my next phase of research. Amado and Juan Luis had suggested that this time we meet in Lima, and from there drive up into the coastal desert of northern Peru, to the ruins at Chavín[1] de Huántar,[2] a small rural village located in a fertile valley on the eastern slope of the Cordillera Blanca, the highest section of the Peruvian Andes. Chavín de Huántar is also referred to as "San Pedro de Chavín" (Rowe, 1967), and, according to Amado and Juan Luis, it is here that the San Pedro cactus had its beginnings as a ritual tool.[3]

For Juan Luis, Chavín has special significance, for it is the sacred center of the Medicine teachings in which he was trained.

Juan Luis said, "Chavín[4] is the home of San Pedro, which is the Medicine with which I work. It is the place of my cosmic and spiritual origins on this Mother Earth. I have an absolute connection with Chavín. I am part of Chavín and Chavín is part of me. All the knowledge that I can achieve in this life, consciously and unconsciously, comes from Chavín. As a place of birth, I am born there every time I go."

"In all of the Americas, this is probably the most ancient culture, the Chavín people. All our great-grandchildren will always know that that was the center, that that was the place where these lineages could meet again. [Chavín] is the meeting point. Our planet was basically created with the wisdom and the life that was brought from the cosmos in [Chavín]. That's the center. It is the strongest place of *yanantin-masintin*, for it is capable of creating new humanity if we are talking about humanity, or new life, or new levels of life in the planet, in the cosmos."

Later, Amado spoke further about Chavín, saying, "Chavín is the place where a cosmic seed was planted—where the Medicine was brought from the cosmos to this earth. You see, we have legends that say that the Medicine was brought from the stars, and, in fact, when the San Pedro plant is cut into [horizontal] slices, it has the shape of starflowers. The Medicine arrived first to Chavín. Thousands of years later, there was supposed to be another energetic center created, another Chavín for these new times, for this new era. That center was Qosqo [Cuzco]. But the original center of spiritual centers was Chavín. This is where the Medicine began. All the work with *ayahuasca, huachuma,*[5] *vilca*[6]—all these sacred medicines that allow you to enter into higher-level dimensions of light began here.

"In all of history we will always learn that Chavín is the mother culture. Why? Because all our life as an Andean people is rooted in our spirituality—in our connection to Mother Earth and to the cosmos. Chavín held all that spiritual connection. The most inaccessible people were those who came from Chavín lineage. Sechin, Chan Chan, north of Sipán—all these places were not easily influenced by the Inca civilization. They knew very well that the Inca did not hold all the spiritual roots, and because of that they kept their own culture. Because for life to continue, to survive, they knew that more important than food, more important than water, was this spiritual connection. Only through that could they work with the elements, with Mother Earth, in perfect harmony. It was to that that their life was promised."

Most Chavín scholars (Bischof, 2008; Burger, 1995; Cordy-Collins, 1977; Cummins, 2008; Rick, 2008; Rowe, 1967) agree that, in its heyday, the Chavín site was likely a place of important ritual activity. Although the dates are debated, it is believed to have been in active use as early as 1500 BCE to around 200 BCE (Conklin & Quilter, 2008). Some (Burger, 1995; Rowe, 1967) believe that Chavín de Huántar was the origin and sacred center of a religious cult that spread across central and northern Peru from about 1300 BCE to 800 BCE. These scholars speculate that the force of Chavín's religious momentum was such that it was able to unite the various cultures of the area—once composed of various disparate groups—by a common ideology and set of religious practices, so much so that at its apex in the last millennium BCE, Chavín culture had linked groups across much of the central and northern coast and highlands of Peru. Of course, this, too, is debated.

The buildings that are currently visible at the ruins of Chavín de Huántar include an asymmetrical system of pyramids, plazas, and platforms. The oldest structure at the site is a U-shaped pyramidal platform called the "Old Temple" (which contrasts with a newer section of the building referred to as the "New Temple"). Isbell suggested that the U-shape of the Old Temple expressed the "opposing and yet complementary forces within society and the cosmos" and that "the central building at the apex of the U represents the synthesis of these opposing forms. In this view, the plaza becomes a neutral field mediating between opposing cosmic domains, while the center of the central mound is the critical point of synthesis and resolution" (as cited in Burger, 1995, pp. 62–63).

Joralemon and Sharon (1993) consider the temple complex to be "a cosmic center in which opposites were mediated and balance was maintained through the performance of appropriate religious ceremonies" (p. 183).

The Old Temple contains a series of subterranean tunnels and galleries. At the center of this labyrinth sits the Lanzón, a 15-foot carved granite monolith believed to represent the Chavín cult's principal deity. Given its position, scholars (Burger, 1995; Cummins, 2008) surmise that the Old Temple was constructed with the specific purpose of enshrining the Lanzón.

It has been suggested (Burger, 1995; Joralemon & Sharon, 1993; Rick, 2008) that the entire complex at Chavín de Huántar was designed with the intent of manipulating the consciousness of those who entered it. It is generally believed that this otherworldly ambience was intended to provoke a "highly orchestrated phenomenological experience" (Cummins, 2008, p. 282) that would affect the ritual participant's state of consciousness in a way that gave one the sensation of stepping out of ordinary, sensate reality and into sacred space and time.

Rick (2008) noted,

The very nature of the architecture of Chavín—with its sunken plazas and towering buildings—cut off much of the view of the outside world, and the decidedly divorced underground world of the galleries was aimed at creating a "place apart," where normal experience would be suspended, perhaps in an emulation of shamanistic other-world experience. (p. 32)

The artwork discovered at Chavín de Huántar is likewise considered highly religious in nature and is believed to express themes of harmony and balance between the opposites.[7] A carving found at Chavín shows the Lanzón deity holding a Strombus shell in its right hand and a Spondylus shell in its left, which Burger (1995) suggested is "a metaphor for its role in balancing the male and female forces of the universe" (p. 174). Similarly, Stone-Miller (2002) pointed to recurring patterns of interlocked opposites, pairs, doubling, mirror imaging, and light and shadow oppositions found in the artwork of this region as reflecting the importance of complementarity. For example, carvings found in the north coastal area of Peru, when inverted, reveal a second, hidden figure. This dedication to representing the "two in one" or duality in oneness, wrote Stone-Miller (2002), "created interesting artistic challenges such as how to show two things as one or existence beyond terrestrial space" (p. 16).

Chavín iconography is also famous for its practice of combining the features of two or more different creatures into one hybrid being. For example, the mouth of any creature, human or otherwise, is often represented with long, pointed canines overlapping the lips. Felines, birds, and serpents[8] are all common elements out of which these anthropomorphic figures are composed. Burger (1995) pointed out that "most of the Chavín figures are monstrous, both in the sense of being terrifying and in the sense of combining features which do not occur together in nature" (p. 148). Some scholars (Rowe, 1967) argued that these hybrid creatures are meant to represent supernatural beings. Others (Burger, 1995; Cordy-Collins, 1977) suggested that they represent San Pedro ecstasies in which the ritual participant makes a transformation from human to animal.

Amado offered his own opinion on this debate. "Both are true," he insisted. "Because when these supernatural beings connect to you, they are transmitting their essence into you. While you are a human being, you are also the completely integrated consciousness of, say, the hawk that represents seeing far, or the puma that is completely connected to this earth, or the serpent that travels through consciousness just like water travels through a river. In a way, you do become all this by receiving the essence of these beings. So both are part of the truth. Both are accessing important parts of this experience."

It is generally agreed (Bischof, 2008; Burger, 1995; Rick, 2008; Rowe, 1967) that the "visual confusion" (Burger, 1995, p. 147) created by the Chavín artwork was meant to induce altered states of consciousness on the part of the viewer.

Burger (1995) commented,

> All religious art is based ultimately on analogy and metaphor, but Chavín artists made this principle the cornerstone of their style, spinning visual metaphor into a web so complex that many find the end product incomprehensible. Yet even modern viewers find that the best of Chavín art succeeds in evoking the sensation of being in the presence of something extraordinary. (p. 202)

Or, as Rowe (1967) put it, "It is a religious art, but it is also a highly intellectual one, produced for people who were willing to have their minds challenged as well as their emotions" (p. 86).

"Yes! Yes, yes, yes!" Amado agreed when I read him Rowe's statement. "They wanted the mind confused! They wanted it lost! They wanted it completely in frustration! They want it completely challenged . . . all over. They wanted it completely empty. That's why the labyrinths were put [inside the Old Temple]. They'll pull your mind apart! And only one thing finally puts it back together. Once you go through this labyrinth and arrive to where the Lanzón is—the Lanzón who is the Master of Masters—ultimately what is challenged is nothing less than your life-beating heart. Your emotions. Everything that is in you. At that point you are not your mind anymore because they had already taken care of the mind."

"Mind challenging" was certainly the effect the complex at Chavín had on me. Amado and Juan Luis were right to bring me there. One did not even need to have ingested San Pedro to feel as though one had been thrust into an altered state of consciousness. That sense of liminality was embedded in every stone upon which these images had been carved.

That went doubly so for the Lanzón.

The Lanzón.

My god, the Lanzón.

Rowe (1967) described the Lanzón (also called "The Great Image" and "The Smiling God") as a "cult image of major importance" and "one of the few cult objects of ancient Peruvian religion which can still be seen in its original setting" (p. 75). The Lanzón is a shaft of white granite of almost 15 feet long. It has a notched upper section, giving it a knifelike appearance. It is believed by some (Burger, 1995; Cummins, 2008) to be a representation of the axis mundi, the center pillar that connects all three levels of the Andean cosmos.[9] This theory is reinforced by its design. The shaft penetrates the roof and the floor of the temple, symbolizing its connection to the *hanaq pacha*, *kay pacha*, and *ukhu pacha*. The carving upon it is that of a being with large upper fangs and a snarling mouth of a feline combined with the torso, ears, legs, and hands of a human being.[10] Its right arm is raised with the open palm exposed. Its left arm is lowered so that only the back of the hand is visible—a pose that Burger suggested expresses its role as "a mediator of opposites, a personification of the principle of balance and order" (as cited in Joralemon & Sharon, 1993, p. 183). The being's hair and eyebrows are represented as snakes, and its tunic is belted with a row of heads.

Amado explained the Lanzón this way: "The deity that is represented in the Lanzón—the essence that it holds, the spirit that it carries—is not of this planet. It is not human. It is a being of a whole different dimension of life, of existence. A cosmic gardener, as we call it. The Medicine had to be brought by somebody from the stars, and we believe that that somebody looked like the Lanzón."

Juan Luis told me, "The Lanzón for us in this path means the semen, that sperm that arrived from the cosmos and hit the egg—the egg being Pachamama. It created for the whole planet the meeting of elements and the meeting of the elementals. With the help of the four elements, it started creating the whole world, the whole culture of humanity. Some people call it the axis mundi because it is the sacred knowledge. For us, that is the center, especially in the spiritual world. That is why there is a whole culture that has been developed around it which is based only in spirituality."

Before leaving for the trip, I had seen pictures of the Lanzón in books. But nothing prepared me for what it was to see it in person. It was awful—and by that I mean "awful" in the original and truest sense of the word as something that makes one feel "full of awe."

At the end of September, I arrived in Lima, Peru's capital. My first day there was spent trying to recover my lost luggage and sleeping off the effects of jetlag. On the afternoon of the second day, Amado and Juan Luis arrived at my hotel. They had brought Amado's uncle, Ernesto, to help with the driving and also because he had never been to the northern desert before and had always wanted to see it. We rented a car and the four of us headed north. I found myself utterly enchanted by the stark beauty of the seemingly endless desert. Precipitation in this area rarely exceeds one inch per year, and for miles there were only barren stretches of desert, a muted landscape painted in soft pastels of pink and gold and blue gray. Dunelike mountains rose up out of the long stretches of sand and shale. Every now and then we would catch glimpses of gleaming, snow-capped *apus* in the distance. With the glimmering white juxtaposed against the dun-colored sands of the desert, it felt like another world: A world outside of a world outside. A dream within a dream. A double fugue.

The drive up the steep mountain road into the town of Chavín was slow and treacherous. There had been a number of rockslides, and the road was littered with debris ranging from small stones that we could simply drive over to large boulders that sent us swerving sickeningly close to the edge. At around 4:00 that afternoon, we arrived at our hotel. By the time we checked in and unloaded the car it was close to 5:00. As we arrived at the ruins, the tourists were being graciously but firmly herded out of the gates. Amado managed to slip through and disappeared for a short while. He came back having arranged with the caretaker to let us enter the site early the next morning. We would do ceremony there, he told me.

"Will we take San Pedro while we are inside?" I asked.

Juan Luis shook his head and said, "In Chavín, the vibration is much too powerful. It is at the level that you don't have to take San Pedro to feel it. The energy of the Medicine is there already. The shock could be too strong when you are connecting with the Lanzón if you were with the Medicine. The remedy could be worse than the illness."

He then added, "When we are in Chavín, we *are* the Medicine."

As the four of us walked back to the hotel from the site, I found myself suddenly exhausted and feverish. I had a headache and my throat felt swollen. Knowing we would be getting up early the next morning, I excused myself and went to bed. I slept poorly that night. My dreams were unsettled and unsettling. In one, I was reading a newspaper and found an article about my grandmother, who was being acknowledged for having done some important social work in her community. My grandmother had been dead for more than 20 years, and while I was happy to discover that she was alive, I was upset that no one told me that she had returned from the land of the dead. In the next dream, I received an urgent message to fly home right away. A friend picked me up at the airport and, on our way home, killed a bicyclist who crossed suddenly in front of the car.

Such strange, haunting images of life and death.

I woke up in a sweat and barely slept the rest of the night. By the time 4:00 a.m. rolled around, I felt completely drained, both physically and emotionally. Dragging myself downstairs, I met Amado and Juan Luis in the hotel courtyard. When we tried to leave, we discovered that the hotel's front gate was locked, and we were trapped inside. The three of us spent the next 20 minutes trying to find the hotel *dueña*. She eventually emerged, looking completely annoyed with us.

The caretaker and his dog met us at the entrance to the ruins. The dog followed closely behind us as we made our way toward the western side. By now it was almost 5:00, and the morning light was just starting to illuminate the sky, creating a surreal glow that bounced off the granite, sandstone, and limestone blocks of the temple walls.

We walked along the outer perimeter to the southwestern corner of the temple. The wall here was once adorned with a row of elaborately carved stone faces. Now only one remains in place while the rest are preserved in the site's small museum. Burger (1995) speculated that, when put in their original order, the "tenon heads"[11] depict a shaman's transformation from human to animal. He noted that the heads were positioned in such a way that they would have been the first sight encountered by a visitor arriving at the temple. As we passed, the remaining head stared down at us from its position high up on the wall.

The three of us continued around the complex, finally ending up at what is referred to as the "Rectangular Sunken Court"—a below-ground-level plaza with short staircases leading into it. Amado and Juan Luis stopped at the entrance and closed their eyes.

I waited.

A moment later, Juan Luis said in a low voice, "The Masters have arrived."

The words had barely left his lips when the caretaker's dog let out a long, slow whimper. The hairs on the back of my neck stood up. And then, from across the complex, came a strange, high-pitched chirping sound—something like a bird might make. A really, really *big* bird.

I jumped.

"What the fuck was that?"

Amado looked at Juan Luis. Juan Luis shrugged and glanced around, squinting in the hazy light. A moment later, the sound came again, louder this time and . . . was it just my imagination? . . . more urgently.

"Jesus!" I said, jumping for the second time. We all jerked our heads around in the direction of the sound. Amado grabbed my arm and pointed to the flat-topped, terraced platform above the temple. Standing there, looking straight at us, was a llama. It parted its lips and made the strange howling-chirping noise for the third time.

"I've never heard a llama make a noise like that," I said.

"Me neither," Amado said, and then added, "maybe only that one does."

Juan Luis instructed me to go to the center of the sunken plaza. "Introduce yourself to the Masters," he told me. He and Amado would meet me on the other side when I was through. The two of them walked around the plaza to the other side. Unsure of what exactly I was supposed to do, I descended the stairway into the courtyard, then walked toward the center and waited. After a few moments, I suddenly felt feverish and weak again, as if I were being pulled downward by gravity. I knelt down and put my head on the ground between my hands. When I felt light again, I stood up and walked across the court, ascending the stairs on the other side.

The light was a little stronger now. The sky was no longer dark charcoal but a hazy blue-pink-gray, making everything appear muted and blurry. I spotted two figures off in the near distance and, assuming they were Amado and Juan Luis, began to walk toward them, away from the temple. A trio of llamas—there were three of them on the hill now—began screeching. Not the strange chirping like before, but this time a synchronized bellow. I realized then that the figures I had seen were not Amado and Juan Luis but were two workers starting their day. Amado and Juan Luis were standing at the eastern side of the New Temple just below the llamas. Had the llamas not screeched at me, I would have gone in the wrong direction.

I walked up next to them. They were standing in front of the Black and White Stone Portal, a bicolored stairway framed by two columns composed of carved black limestone and white granite. Upon each column was carved the figure of a human-raptor-feline hybrid.

Burger (1995) wrote,

> As we have seen, complementary opposition remained at the heart
> of Chavín cosmology. The carved columns of the Black and White
> Portal illustrate the way in which this theme was expressed in the
> iconography of public constructions. . . . The theme of duality is
> emphasized by carving half the lintel in white granite and half in
> black limestone. (pp. 175–176)

Seeing the intricate carvings, I exclaimed, "Oooooh!" and reached out
to touch one of them. As I did so, Juan Luis grabbed my arm and pulled
me back, shaking his head in a scolding manner. I looked at him, startled.
He bowed his head and motioned for me to do the same. I felt ashamed,
like a child who had to be taught how to behave properly in the face of
such things.

Finally, they walked me over to the entrance of the Old Temple. Inside
the Old Temple is a labyrinth of narrow passageways, subterranean cham-
bers, ventilation ducts, and canals. With Amado and Juan Luis waiting
outside, I stepped through the door. The entire temple structure was without windows, an architectural feature that I did not fully appreciate until
I stepped inside. If the lack of lighting and the narrow passageways were
designed intentionally in order to, as Burger (1995) suggested, "create a
sense of confusion and disorientation in which the individual is severed
from the outside world" (p. 135), then it produced this experience absolutely.
It was as if the whole setting conspired to propel one out of the comforts of
habitual consciousness and into some strange liminal space. It was about
five degrees warmer inside the temple, and although I am not typically
claustrophobic, I found myself wanting to leave immediately.

The temple's main passageway takes one partially underground. After
walking a short distance, I took a left into the dark corridor leading to the
Lanzón. The tunnel is almost 40 feet long and only a little over three feet
wide—so narrow that only one person can walk down the passageway at a
time. I walked down the passageway slowly, inhaling the smell of stagnant
earth. At the end of the tunnel was a metal gate that separates the viewer
from the Lanzón by a distance of about two feet. I knelt in front of it.

Rowe (1967) wrote that the Lanzón has "an awe-inspiring quality which
can be felt even by a present-day unbeliever" (p. 75). This was putting it

mildly. For me, it was like seeing something out of a nightmare. Logically, I couldn't say why it had such a profound effect. Certainly, the Lanzón's face with its fangs and strange hybrid expression was eerie, but my reaction was totally unexpected and completely nonrational. The only way I can describe what it was to sit there in front of it is that looking at it was like trying to stare directly into the sun. Kneeling there, I had the sense that if I were to spend too much time with it, something inside me might be obliterated, might collapse from the power of it. An eclipse of the soul might occur that would be too much for my psyche to handle.

It was incredible, but horrible. Horrible, but incredible. I turned my head away from it, now only looking at it from my peripheral vision. Juan Luis appeared behind me and began to whisper something that I could not understand. I have no idea how long I was in there, but when Juan Luis instructed me to return, I wasted no time in getting out of there, scrambling out backward, afraid to turn my back on it.

Outside, the sun was now rising fast, and the sky was lit up like an explosion. I sat down on a rock, catching my breath.

Amado said nothing.

Juan Luis said nothing.

I said nothing.

The dog curled up against Juan Luis's feet.

We watched the sun come up over the hills.

"What was your experience, Princesa?" Amado asked, finally.

The light was hitting Amado's face in a way that made him look like a golden statue. Juan Luis leaned over and scratched the dog behind the ears.

I told them about how it felt being in there—my desire to get out, and the difficulty I had even looking at it because of the sense that it might destroy some essential part of me.

"Why would I have that reaction?" I asked them, feeling self-conscious.

"You were supposed to have that reaction," Amado told me. "That is what Chavín was designed for. When the labyrinths were in use, many would not even make it alive to the Lanzón."

"Why?"

"Because in that process in the labyrinth with the Medicine it could easily get to the point that the automatic work of your body—you need to breathe, you need to hydrate, you need to whatever—would also be gone. So, you leave and never come back to your body anymore."

"Its face," I said, looking back at the entrance to the Old Temple and suppressing a small shudder. "And not just the face—the whole thing, actually. There was something about it that hit me so deeply. Something that touched some core, primitive part of me. Some deep fear, I guess."

Before either of them could respond, I shook my head.

"No. That's not exactly right. It wasn't fear that I felt, but . . . something else. I really don't have a word for it. Dread, maybe?"

Amado nodded. "The Lanzón is a being that has the power to take your limited mentality, so that you can access all dimensions of life and all levels of consciousness, so that you can then be of best service here on this planet. You saw how the Lanzón has been built in the shape of a knife?" he asked. "For a lot of people, here they receive that striking knife of the cosmos that will cut whatever negative vibration, whatever heavy energy, whatever suffering and struggle you carry. As it is cutting, it is healing. You know? When it cuts, it is opening a whole new layer of life that is much deeper, that is much purer. Perhaps that is what you were feeling."

"And that is a beautiful thing," Juan Luis said. "Today, in ceremony here in Chavín, I felt a beautiful recognition of how we are part of this great path, this great journey. The biggest satisfaction for me is to see the eyes opening of the people that are beginning in this path—to witness that awakening. What greater honor than to open the eyes and wake up in such a place? Although it is not a place that is famous and not very well known by a lot of people, that is actually what allows it to keep its essence pure."

The tourists were beginning to trickle in. It was time to leave. I followed Amado and Juan Luis back through the site and back into the square. We found Uncle Ernesto sitting on a bench in front of the hotel, and the four of us went to a nearby restaurant for breakfast.

FIGURE 9: © Carl A. Hyatt, 2005, Don Maximo, Cuzco

CHAPTER SEVEN

On Good and Evil; Life and Death

I THOUGHT ABOUT MY EXPERIENCE with the Lanzón the rest of that day and into the next. I couldn't get over the reaction that I, a "rational Westerner," had experienced sitting there in front of it—that combined sense of awe and dread that was like nothing I had ever felt before. Amado referred to the Lanzón as something that cuts in order to heal. It seemed that just as with the *tinkuy* battles, the discomfort I felt in front of the Lanzón was part of an intentional process that, while uncomfortable, was intended to have a positive outcome.

Burger (1995) noted the following about the Lanzón:

> Its upturned mouth, enlarged upper canines and elongated sharpened nails on its hands and feet dispel any doubt about its ferocity. Yet the pose of the deity seems to depict him in the process of preserving the balance of the cosmos. The reconciliation of opposites and the maintenance of cosmic harmony were probably believed to hold the key to the stability of Chavín society, as well as the continued fertility of crops and animals. (p. 150)

All this got me thinking, got me wondering, about the two core dichotomous pairs that we human beings deal with—that of "good and evil" and "life and death." The next day, as we wound our way out of Chavín, I asked Amado and Juan Luis for their perspectives on these issues.

Amado began. "According to the beliefs of the Andean cosmovision, there is no such thing as good or bad," he said. "What happens is there is negative and positive, there is male and female. Always that duality. And when a person looks at it from a two-dimensional world, either of them is possible to change at all times. Whatever is positive can be negative in a moment. Whatever is negative can be positive in a moment. It's not like heaven is heaven and hell is hell. In the Andean cosmovision these things can be changed very quickly."

He smiled knowingly at me. "This part is very delicate, because while it is very easy to say, for a person who is just opening their mind to this kind of thing, it can be a shock to hear. It's a little bit hard to explain how that specifically works. And yet that is what I experience. In a healing, for example, I change heavy energy to positive just like that."

He snapped his fingers. "Perhaps I even have the ability to turn positive energy into negative just like that. But because I am aware of what that can create, I don't do that."

"Is 'negative' energy the same as 'evil' energy?" I asked.

"For us, 'evil' is nothing more and nothing less than trickster *apus*. Because when you are arriving to the essence of a human being, of a mountain, of an animal, or of any being, it is not their limitation, it is not their judgments, it is not their fears that we know now as 'devil.' But it can present itself in appearance as that in order to challenge you. You have to have both. You have to have that which you know, and that which you don't know."

"What do you mean by that?" I asked.

"In other words, you have to acknowledge the trickster energy but not be illusioned by it. Instead, you must acknowledge the essence of it."

"The essence of it?"

"The essence of that trickster energy is not what we usually perceive at first. Usually we perceive the surface part of it—what one might think of as 'evil'—and that is what we stick with. Often, a lot of people get lost in the reaction of it, and that reaction creates a blockage that keeps you from accessing it deeper. So, out of fear, out of irritation, you react to it.

But the essence is much deeper. It is something that you have to journey into further."

He saw my confused look. "What I mean is, for example, if [another shaman] does some sorcery work against us, we don't react, because reacting is just playing into the surface part of that trickster energy. When we are facing that trickster energy, our first response is usually fear or pain or anger—all that heavy stuff. But once the first impression is done, what is your next action? Some people would choose to try and send that heavy energy back to whomever sent it to them, but, in my personal opinion, you don't need to do that. You don't *want* to do that. If you open yourself up to it, that *hucha* that is being sent can be the best gift for you! Because that heavy energy is free energy given by that person, even if it was sent out of jealousy or envy or whatever. Instead, you can use that energy for yourself. It is the best wisdom, the best secret of life. So, we journey into the deeper essence of it and use it to feed projects, to make healings . . . anything. If we go deeper into it, we will eventually find out what its teaching is—for example, why it is coming to us at this point in our lives, how is it serving us, how is it helping us in our service with the world? So, if you send it back to the person, you should send it back as gratitude, because it is free energy that you didn't ask for that, now, thanks to that person, is coming to you. It is free energy being given!"

"I like that idea," I said. "But, of course, that kind of thing is always easier said than done. Getting past that first reaction, I mean. How do we do that?"

"You have to be a warrior," said Amado. "Every second, every minute of our lives we are to be warriors of light. It's okay to have that first reaction and, yes, maybe even be afraid or angry. That's natural. But then you must open up more and ask, 'What is this all about?' Go deeper. We need to know the darkness and respect it as well. Not to take it for granted.

"That was part of my training with Grandfather," Amado said. "A lot of times, Grandfather would ask me, 'What would you do if . . . ?' Or, 'How would you react if . . . ?' Because to react is easy, but to put into action who you are is much more delicate. Like, for example, he would say to me, 'What do you do when you are being challenged by a friend in school? What do you do?' I would say to him, 'Out of love I would do nothing because I don't know what my strength is.' Our strength is infinite. Even if I win, nothing goes one way. That being that I hit is not just the person but, as Grandfather says, is also the soul. We talk at the soul level. That soul would hit you back.

How would you feel then, you know? My actions influence the essence, not just the form or the shape."

"So," I asked him, "do you mean that during your training there was a lot of learning how to work with your own energies so that you are not as tempted to go from your first reaction—for example, anger or fear or that kind of thing—which might be the root of sorcery?"

"Right! It is so easy to react, so easy to come out of the frustration or the anger. Those trickster *apus* are very powerful. That's why they are very important in the Andes, much like Coyote in the North. A lot of healers in the Andes, when they meet with these trickster *apus*, they close themselves up very fast. They've never really understood the deeper essence, so they go on being tricksters themselves."

"But just so I'm clear," I said slowly, trying to tease this apart in my mind, "are you saying that things that some people might consider 'evil'—for example, murder, rape, genocide—all that is the work of a 'trickster *apu*'?"

"Yes," Amado answered. "You ask about murder. In the Andes, there were very specialized murderers. There were these people called the *ñak'aq*, who were the most specialized killers. They would go on the mountain, find somebody who was passing by, and . . ."

Amado drew his finger across his neck in a slicing gesture.

"Good-bye!"

He paused, waiting for my reaction.

"And that's okay?" I asked, cautiously.

"It doesn't matter if it is okay or not, because if the cosmos says this person is not supposed to die, then no one—not a *ñak'aq* or anybody—can take him. If he does die, if he is murdered, then that is the energy that the cosmos used to liberate the person from his physical limitations. Everyone is interwoven with the cosmos in order to be who they are, even those people who are doing these rapes and murders. It is almost at a level where you have to support them, at least with a prayer."

I must have looked shocked at what he was saying, because he smiled slightly.

"You might think I am crazy, but you have to!" he said. "You have to because imagine the weight the murderer or rapist has to carry. Look at George [W.] Bush. Yes! Let's talk about George Bush. Imagine the heavy energy that he has to carry. Poor guy, really, because of all the heaviness that he has to carry for being who he is. You see, this life we carry . . . it's almost like God is telling you, 'Welcome to the movie. What part do you want to play? What part of this drama do you want to play? Do you want to be the bad guy or the good guy?' And then you have to choose. Or maybe you don't have a choice! Maybe you *have* to be the bad guy. Instead, God says, 'Do you want to be the bad guy? Yes, or yes?'"

I laughed.

"Or," Amado continued. "'Do you want to be the good guy? Yes, or yes?' It's all part of the cosmic program, and if you become a little bit bad when you are supposed to be good, you get kicked around. And if you become good when you are supposed to be bad, you get kicked around, too."

Juan Luis had been silent throughout our exchange, but now he twisted around in his seat to face us.

"Even these murderers have a mission," he said. "That's exactly right. The level of justice or injustice, of good and evil—that is only seen by the eyes of the human being. For the eyes of God, that person—the murderer or the kidnapper or the assassin—might actually be fulfilling his mission of love. Like when we speak of Judas's betrayal of Master Jesus. Judas's spirit had to be bigger than the Master Jesus's spirit in order to betray him, in order to take on such a big weight."

"Hold on, though!" I said. "Are you saying that we must love and accept all things? Even those things that are destructive to ourselves or others?"

Juan Luis shook his head. "No. Not that. In this world, only the crazy people would say, 'I am not against the bad.' But you have to be against the bad in a very harmonious way."

"So, if you saw something that you considered bad or evil and you had the opportunity to stop it, you would?" I asked them.

They both looked shocked at my question.

"Of course!" Amado said. "If it is in our hands? Oh yeah! Yeah, yeah, *yeah*. No doubt. No thinking twice about it. But then, again, how do I know what's right or wrong? First, you have to know how to recognize it. First, you have to know the dark side and the light side of it all."

"It's like with the *mesa*," Juan Luis said. "One side is light and the other side is dark. On one side we put knives, swords, and on the other we put staffs. A person who walks this path must know both sides of the mesa. *Must*. In order to heal."

"After all," Juan Luis continued, "what is the difference between a shaman and a *brujo* [sorcerer]? The *brujo* knows a lot of tricks in order to do his work. But the shaman is a channel. He has a direct connection with the cosmos and Mother Earth. It is in the heart of each person to decide what we do with our lives. It is very easy for us to use our powers or our knowledge in order to take advantage. Then we lose it. All of that—what we want to use that knowledge for—is in our heart and is our choice. How do we use what we know?"

I thought about this for a moment. "There's a debate in Western philosophy that questions whether we are free to choose our own path or if our lives are already preplanned by some higher force," I offered. "Listening to you, I feel like I'm hearing both things at once. So, which is it? Is it personal choice or is it Cosmic Will?"

"We always have a choice," Juan Luis said. "We are changing things by the second. Imagine how responsible we are for the energy we move in ceremony! Nevertheless, the Cosmic Will is more consciously involved in it than we are."

Amado interjected, "Grandfather always used to tell me that this is where a lot of healers get off track. It happens almost at a level where they won't notice until they can't come back anymore."

"Can't come back?"

"This is a very delicate path," he said. "There is a lot of power in these teachings, and a lot of great medicine men and women get lost. They become sorcerers. That is not the path of love and light. It is not the path of a warrior. The heaviness becomes in control of you. During my training, I would say to Grandfather, 'I want to learn all the different ways of making a *despacho*.' For example, a *wisq'a despacho*, which is how to block heaviness that someone has sent you, or a *cuti despacho*, which is how to send back a curse that someone has sent you. Or, for another example, how to split couples, how to get them together, or how to make families get better or make them worse. When I asked him to show me this, Grandfather said to me, 'Knowing what that involves, you want to make these *despachos*?' And I said to Grandfather, 'Well, yes, so that I can at least recognize when somebody is doing something.' Then Grandfather said to me, 'All I have to tell you is that some people will do a million *despachos* in order to arrive to the point, to the level, where their life is the *despacho*. Where *they* are the offering. Where *they* can be the best offering for the family, for the community, for Mother Earth.'"

Juan Luis nodded in agreement.

"In other words," Amado said, "he was telling me to be careful with doing a lot of rituals, because you are already in ceremony always. So, not to take it for granted. For me, that has been very powerful training. Because whether I am with Grandfather in ceremony, or whether I am traveling from the mountains to New York City and drinking a martini in a bar, or whether I am dancing hip-hop in a club in San Francisco, all of that is part of the ceremony. It is part of my training. It is part of my mission to continue doing my healing at levels that maybe my conscious mind is too limited to grasp."

I considered this. A thought occurred to me. "What do you believe happens after death?" I asked them.

Amado and Juan Luis both chuckled.

"At death, it is almost hard for consciousness to realize that you are no longer in your physical body," Juan Luis said. "When it happens, oftentimes you don't even know you have changed vibration or frequency. You are in life living happily without noticing anything, then all of a sudden you see your family, you see your community, you are going into your kitchen, but nobody is talking to you anymore. Nobody is looking at you anymore. No one can see you physically. A long time ago such a thing would not happen. A whole community, a whole family was trained to see a person even when they have left their physical body, so that when you are leaving, they are slowly acclimatizing you to not being in your physical temple anymore. Back then, you would enter into your house and everyone would still say 'Hello, Princesa, how are you?' They would acknowledge your spirit, your essence. It would be as if you were still there, even if you are not there physically anymore. This was training that they used to get since they were children. But nowadays, we no longer have that training, so death is a shock for the consciousness, for the spirit."

"In ceremony with San Pedro, I had an experience with death," Juan Luis said. "From then on, I understood that I don't need to fear it, but rather I have a lot of respect for it. Often we are afraid of what we don't know. But when you know it, there is nothing to fear. Death is our opportunity to transcend from this physical level to a higher, spiritual level. So, for me, death means to transcend to another level of consciousness."

"Death is for us the rebirth," Amado said. "We spend our whole life-time in the womb in preparation to be born. Like so, this life is only a preparation. At death, we will be born into a new life. The reason why you leave this physical body is because you are ready for a new frequency of energy that your body cannot handle."

Juan Luis said, "There is a great reality that for me is a great truth as well. And that is this: Every night when we go to sleep, we die. That's why we should give thanks to every new day. Every day is a gift, a new life, for that consciousness. We would say that nobody actually leaves. The doorway of entrance is the exit, and the exit is the entrance."

I said, "I suppose that if you believe that death is not the end of everything, if you believe that it is just the end of one cycle and the beginning of another, then the idea of murder loses its negative connotation—at least somewhat. I mean, on one level I can get that, but on another it feels very hard for me to accept."

"But imagine, in ancient cultures, people used to prepare their whole lifetime for death!" Amado said. "They knew that every second of our existence here was affecting eternity. Imagine a young girl of 13 years old journeying for hundreds of kilometers down to the high mountains of Argentina with her braids and her offerings. Imagine her sitting down in one of the crevasses and choosing to give her life as an offering to all the gods in the name of her community and family. Hundreds of years later, when she is found again, she is still the offering. That is service! At some point, consciousness doesn't recognize death anymore. When you can access that, you no longer perceive death either at the beginning or at the end of some cycle. Such a powerful realization! Only then will you acknowledge your departure from this physical plane differently. We are always in our journey back home. In the meantime, we are put here to serve."

"Serve? In what way?" I asked.

"Our service is to that which we have to take care of in this lifetime."

"Like karma?"

Amado shook his head. "We do not believe in karma in the way that the Hindu people believe in it. We believe in the kind of karma you find here in this world as the result of biological connections or because of spiritual lineages. We originally come here pure. But heaviness, that *hucha* . . . you find it here in the *kay pacha* and you take it on right away. You collect it. And that's what you are meant to process in life. And whatever that process is, whether it is hard or soft or easy or difficult, it is done in service for the collective."

"So you *do* believe in reincarnation, but that you come in with a clean slate," I asked.

Amado nodded. "Right. We don't believe in the kind of karma that you can bring into or carry out of this life. It's not like if you don't do it in this lifetime that you have extra to do next time. It is here that we are to take care of it, consciously or unconsciously."

"What happens if you don't finish or complete it?"

"You will," Amado said.

I laughed.

"But what if I don't?"

"You *will*."

"For sure?"

"For sure. That's what you are here for. Even if you don't consciously perceive it, that does not mean you didn't complete it. That's why when you are walking this path you must realize more and more that anything that you are going through that is uncomfortable, that is painful, or that is very difficult—even life threatening—is part of that process. And that's why forgiveness is such a powerful, powerful tool to liberate ourselves. Before forgiveness, there was love. Before guilt there was love. After forgiveness and after the liberation of guilt, there will only be love. Ultimately, love has the last word."

Uncle Ernesto had been silent throughout our entire exchange.

"*Tío*," I asked, poking my chin between the two front passenger seats, "what do you think of all this?"

Continuing to look forward at the road, he said, "Everything that Amado and Juan Luis are speaking about is a reality. The reason why it is a reality is because who is really speaking about these issues is not Amado and Juan Luis, but it is our ancestors."

Then he was silent again. I could think of no more profound a statement to end our conversation.

On a subsequent trip, Juan Luis's teacher, don Ignacio, would echo Amado's words about the Andean perspective on good and evil, telling me, "All this heavy energy is meant to teach us things that we couldn't learn in a loving way. That's it. Simple. There's no Satan or devil. That idea we have created ourselves. . . . We have been taught to blame whatever bad thing that happens to us on this poor being called the devil. While we are suffering so much, this energy must be telling us, 'Why do you blame me for everything? You don't take responsibility for any of it. It has to be all my fault.' You say, 'The devil did this, the devil did that!' and then you can do whatever you want. And when you confess you are all of a sudden for-given—but nobody ever forgives me! I did nothing. I didn't even ask to be created! Why? It's unfair!'"

As a Westerner, I find that, at times, it can be difficult to conceive of such a seemingly morally ambiguous worldview. After all, the core drama of Christianity—the philosophy within which I was raised—is based on the confrontation between opposing principles of good and evil; the forces of creation and destruction; and, correspondingly, those of life and death. To see death simply as a great transformer rather than a thief in the night that steals away the thing that is most precious to us—our life and the lives of those we love—is great in theory, but very difficult to hold onto in the face of it. Did that mean that my Andean participants were free from the pain that results from the passing of a loved one?

Almost a year after our trip to Chavín, in the summer of 2008, Amado's grandfather, his beloved mentor and teacher, died. When I returned in January 2009 for my final fieldwork trip, I asked Amado about Grandfather's last days and also the days following his death. I was curious about how distinctions between life and death played out in "real life," beyond the theory of it. What I learned—or, rather what I was *reminded* of, in a pro-found way—was that the pain that accompanies the passing of a loved one is universal. No matter which model of reality one ascribes to, that pain is part of the human condition from which we cannot escape.

Amado said, "The day before he died my wife said to me, 'Let's go to see Grandfather.' And I was, like, 'No, let him be. Let him have his time. He is always with his children and grandchildren. He needs time for him-self.' But somehow she must have had some intuition because she said, 'No, we're going now.' So, we went to see him. Grandfather was so weak. He said to me, 'Amado, I need to give you the *mesa*.' And I said, 'No, Grandfather, not now.' And Grandfather said, 'Now. It's not going to wait.' He basically crawled from the kitchen into the other house and up the stairs to the sec-ond floor where his altar was. He was so weak. He sat down at the end of the stairway and said, 'Go get the *mesa*!' And I did, and then he gave it to me. At that point, me and Grandfather cried and played the flute. The whole time he was saying, 'Amado, please give my love and blessings to everybody. Continue your path. Be strong. Never give up. Never give up.' He was telling me, 'Remember to listen to yourself first. You must focus on receiving now, not only on giving. Only then can you really give.' All his last teachings were about saying, 'Amado, you are ready. You are not always prepared but you are always ready.' All these beautiful things he said."

Amado's voice became husky.

"Toward the end, Grandfather sent my father for soup, saying that he needed a lot of strength for his journey. He said, 'I only need it for the first part of the journey. After that I will send it back, a thousand times more.' Because we believe that just before the soul completely leaves this realm it has to take care of whatever it didn't complete in this life. The soul journeys to all the places it has been while alive and takes care of all the situations that need to be taken care of. So, the spirit goes to do that. It transcends time. They say that just in minutes the soul can take care of years. But the soul gets very hungry doing this. And very thirsty. Because it doesn't have access to food and water like we do, the soul sometimes takes strength from family, friends, and even those people with whom it has been in situations energetically. Those people become very weak. But when that part is complete and the river is crossed—because the soul has to cross a river—then the person is completely one with the source of vitality and can send it back to anyone that this soul wills: children, grandchildren, family, cousins, people he loved, people he didn't love . . . everybody can receive back. When we pour drinks to Pachamama, when we offer some *kintus* [coca leaf offerings] to the ancestors, to the spirits, to the souls of the dead, we are actually supporting that journey that they have, that mission that they have to complete. It's feeding them. Grandfather must have realized that he was going to need a lot of strength for the beginning part."

Amado took a long slow breath in and then exhaled.

"Do you think he knew it would be his last day?" I asked him.

"I can't take for granted that Grandfather knew, but he was always talking and acting like he did. Grandfather had the most powerful training for that. He was always talking to the family, talking to everybody, as if he was going to leave at any moment. And that way of thinking, of talking, of acting, allowed him to access that space of when he would no longer be here physically. He was always acknowledging the uniqueness of his experiences and never taking it for granted. So, that attitude was preparing him all the time. If he had taken life for granted then he would have had so much fear that he could not have left with such peace, and it would not have allowed him to complete what he was to complete. So, he was in a way training himself in preparation for that. He would always say that 'If I leave today or tomorrow, it is all the same.' Because he would always have the satisfaction that he had completed what he needed to do. That was the main thing. He would always ask me, 'Are you complete? Have you completed everything that you need to do?'"

Amado stopped and took another deep breath. His eyes were filling with tears. I had never seen Amado cry before.

"He left while he was happy, while he was strong, while he saw his family very well and everybody strong. Even energetically he brought us together that last day and gave us his last teachings. And gave me the *mesa*. And then he was prepared. Now when we talk about Grandfather, everyone is joyful. The memories of him are always blessings."

He was silent for a moment. His head dropped to his chest for a moment. He raised it again and let out a great heaving sob.

"But I miss him!" he cried. The tears that had been welling up behind his eyes came spilling out. I sat down next to him and put my arms around him. We held each other. After a few minutes, Amado pulled away and wiped his eyes and face with his sleeve.

"I know Grandfather must be saying, 'Aye, Amado!' But he knows inside my heart I am very happy for him for his healing, for his liberation. But I do miss him," he said, sniffing back the remaining tears. "Still."

"It's a huge rite of passage when your mentor dies," I said.

Amado nodded.

"Yeah. To tell you the truth, the months after that I was feeling lost. After Grandfather's death, in my innocence, I was thinking, 'What now? What now with the *mesa*, now that I carry both forces? What is the next level?' But the beauty of it is that it continues. The magic continues. At even higher levels now. Because then I had the sense of Grandfather telling me, 'Amado, you're thinking of running while you are just taking the first steps.' So, now I just continue. Continue the path."

He looked up at me and put one of his hands on mine.

"Thank you, Princesa, for bringing this medicine. I feel much lighter. I don't share this often. Or even with anybody. I can see that there were still things to lighten."

"Amado," I said, "I am only returning to you the medicine that you have so generously shared with me. After all, nothing ever goes one way, does it?"

It was a phrase that he had said often to me over the last two years, and in that moment, the truth of it hit home for me. We looked at each other deeply and smiled. The smiles turned into soft laughter—the weary laughter of two people who have come face to face with the pain and joy of existence and recognized that, in the end, it is the laughter that keeps us moving through that often soul-wrenching dichotomy.

"No," Amado said. "Nothing ever does. Thank you, Princesa."

FIGURE 10: © Carl A. Hyatt, 1999, Torreón and Apu Yanantin at Machu Picchu

CHAPTER EIGHT

The Symbolic Versus the Actual

─── ◎◎

IN JANUARY 2009, I returned to Cuzco for my final fieldwork trip. I
arrived with a list of the remaining topics that I wanted to cover, among
them the distinction between "symbolic" versus "Actual." This felt like an
essential dichotomy to explore, for the Andean spiritual system is thick
with symbolic vocabulary. Foremost in my mind was the Andean shaman's
mesa, which contains various ritual items, each of which is said to represent a certain energy that can be used within a ritual and/or healing. I had
never really understood the significance that these symbols held for the
practitioners, which made them such an essential aspect of their work. But
I wanted to. I wanted to know what the relationship was between the various spiritual tools and the actual energy that they were said to represent
and even *re-create*.

Truth be told, I had arrived in Peru for that fieldwork trip thinking
that I had already figured it all out, and that all I needed was a few quotes
from my participants to help me support this "understanding" that I had.
Months earlier, during my readings of some of the literature on Andean
philosophy, I had come across a statement by an Andean scholar who, when

critiquing Western "representational thought," wrote, "For the Andean, the *illa* [symbolic representation] of the llama is not a representation of the llama, but actually *is* the llama" and that, therefore, it "makes no sense to speak of the symbol and of the symbolized" (Vasquez, 1998, p. 178). Doing so, he argued, was a purely Western construction, an anthrocentric bias intended to create a rationalist "split" between symbolic action and "real" action, thus accentuating the Western divide between consciousness and reality, mind and matter.

Certainly, the scholar's argument is understandable and likely fueled by a certain frustration at the biases that Western anthropologists have historically brought into the field—biases that imply that symbols are merely products of the psyche rather than having a reality as energies in and of themselves. When cultural "informants" have reported their visionary experiences within dreams or ritual, Western anthropologists have more often than not passed off the content of these visions as metaphors. That is, nonliteral. The reality of the experience is denied, reduced to a psychological stand-in.

This bias is a reflection of how we treat our own visionary experiences. In the West, we analyze dreams to determine what the images "mean" at the psychological level. Perhaps in part we do this to understand, and even to *tame*, the unconscious (and therefore uncontrollable) part of the mind that generates these images. With this assumption as the basis, everything becomes reflective of our own selves. For example, after having a dream of a crow we might ask ourselves, "What part of me does the crow represent?" or "As the crow is a part of me, what message does the crow have for me about me?" Dreaming thus becomes a narcissistic or even solipsistic endeavor, one removed from everything that is not ourselves, a means of controlling the psyche rather than reflecting a reality beyond us.

In contrasting it with the more Western perspective, the aforementioned scholar seemed to be suggesting that within the Andean philosophical model "symbols" are not just symbols but literally *are* the thing that they are meant to represent. Certainly, when considering some of what had come out of my own fieldwork, this idea rang true. When traveling with Amado and Juan Luis, we would often discuss our dreams of the night before. With the two of them, there was never any talk of what the dream meant in an analytical sense. Instead, images within the dream were spoken of as messengers that had an existence beyond our personal worlds, a means by which actual knowledge of the world could be acquired. As Apffel-Marglin (1998) noted, "It is clearly not a matter of speaking metaphorically when they say that Andean peasants converse with the stars, the moon, the plants, the rocks, etc." (p. 26).

The scholar's statement that the *illa* is not *like* the llama but actually *is* the llama fits in very neatly into the dualistic framework that I had been unconsciously developing—a framework that implied that whatever way we in the West do things, in the Andes they must do it opposite (and therefore *better*). Based on that statement, I had become fixated on the idea that while in the West the symbolic is seen as only a stand-in for the thing that it is meant to represent, that in the Andean philosophical model there is no division between the two—that the symbol *is* the thing. Thus convinced, during my interviews, I kept trying to get my participants to confirm this.

Fortunately, they never did give me what I thought I wanted. Because of this, their answer to my questions made little sense to me at first. It was not until, once again, through going into ceremony with San Pedro that I was able to wrench myself out of my own limited construct and receive an answer that was much more subtle and more complex—and therefore felt much more "true"—than the cut-and-dried, polarizing idea that I had become fixated on.

I had decided that one of my first stops during that final fieldwork trip had to be to meet don Ignacio, Juan Luis's teacher, who I had heard so much about. Juan Luis was out of town when I arrived, so Amado came with me and made introductions. We met in don Ignacio's altar room, which held his *mesa*. Don Ignacio's *mesa* was unlike anything I had ever seen before. No shorter than 20 feet long, it was covered in a vast display of icons and ceremonial items. A white-bearded garden gnome complete with red conical hat. Catholic saints for every occasion. A circle of strange hybrid creatures—several of which sported maniacal grins and enormous erections. A ceramic statue of what seemed to be don Quixote on his horse. A plastic fairy from one of the Walt Disney movies. On and on it went with *illas* of all sorts, feathers, animal skins, giant conch shells, crystals, beaded masks, flowers, stones, dried ears of corn, bells.

I took all this in as we sat cross-legged around it. I asked don Ignacio to explain the significance of a *mesa* for his spiritual and healing practices.

"The *mesa* is cosmic reflection of the macro and micro," he told me. "There is a cosmic law that says as it is in the macro, so it is in the micro.

There is that unity. Everything is related. In every instance, in every sacred space, and every field of power, everything is manifested both in the macro and in the micro. In forms, colors, and also figures and elements."

He gestured at his *mesa*. "These items are a reflection of what is in the macro. They give us the facility to use what is in the macro in our daily life. All of it. All that has been manifested, materialized, and that which is yet to manifest. They are instruments of power that we can use for our own benefit or to practice our unconditional service of love."

"My understanding is that the symbol is not just a symbol, but it actually is the thing that it stands for. Is that right?" I asked.

"Yes . . . but, also, no. The symbol is the materialized part. It is like with food when it goes to a laboratory. They can see the chemical and physical aspect of it; they can say, 'It has iron, and it has this protein and that vitamin.' That's the physical part of it. But behind the physical part there is the spirit of it. That is where it becomes unity. You can't just know the symbol and its meaning. You need to enter deeper into the essence of it and find out how you can be of service with that essence in unity with you. At that frequency you can access into the spirit of that symbol. Otherwise, it stays in theory as a sacred symbol. If you don't vibrate with its spirit, vibrating at that intensity, then the symbol is just a symbol."

"What is the relationship between *yanantin* and the *mesa*?" I asked.

"My *yanantin* is a mirror that shows the worst part of me. It's not my contrary, it's my complement, and surely what I need to liberate. So I need to be very grateful then for that reflection. Likewise, in the *mesa* everything is complementary; nothing contradicts or opposes anything. The *mesa* erases the energy of contradiction and transforms it into complementary energy. That's the relation of the *mesa* with *yanantin*. There's not one thing that cannot be *yanantin* there. Not one of these things will produce anything, any result, until you have vibrated into unity with it. That is *yanantin*—to enter into the spirit and the essence of anything that has been materialized. Or of what has been imagined. You must enter into the spirit of it. That's what vibrating into *yanantin* means. That is the essence of *yanantin*."

"The *yanantin* in the *mesa* is always there," Amado added. "It does not accept oppositions, because it is pure essence. That essence is *yanantin*. But when you interact with your *mesa*, that is *masintin*. That's why a *mesa* is very powerful, because through this you can have access to the essence. It's something that you can touch, something that anyone can have access to."

Don Ignacio pointed to the garden gnome. "For example, this elemental being. It's an elemental of Mother Earth. It brings the essence of the child and the innocence of the child or the innocence of the elder as wisdom. How many people have the direct connection with the actual essence in life? Very few. So many of us are not aware or thinking or willing, or at least dreaming of connecting with Mother Earth in a personal way because we are too distracted in life thinking of the future, thinking of our work, or anything. When it is in the *mesa*, it is always connected with the essence."

"So, the symbols help you connect to the essence of whatever it is that you are trying to connect to?" I asked.

"A symbol allows us access to deeper levels," Amado said. "A symbol is the essence manifesting physically to you. And it doesn't matter if you get lost in the symbol, because even then you are still getting the essence directly."

"What do you mean 'lost in the symbol'?"

"Sometimes symbolism can confuse you. However, that confusion is all part of the *tinkuy* process happening between symbol and essence. It is all part of the *masintin* that comes out of that *yanantin* relationship. Some systems make it hard, so hard that the symbols become not only distracting but, worse, misleading. *Misleading.* That's the worst thing, when it is not just distracting you but actually misleading you from the essence. That is important to know. Because how do you recognize when you are working with this symbolism if you are being misled and not just distracted? Being distracted is okay. It happens to all of us. In fact, it's part of the fun. It's part of the game. That is *tinkuy.* That is *masintin.* You are here to live all of that. But to be *misled* . . . that is different."

I waited. And, finally, looking back and forth from Amado to don Ignacio, I said, "So, then, tell me, how do we know if we are being misled?"

"Only by listening to yourself," don Ignacio said. "Because something, when you are no longer in harmony, will know. Something will always know. And it will let you know. It's just a process. And it doesn't have to be hard. That's the thing! It doesn't have to be hard."

I left this conversation not feeling as if too much had been cleared up for me. But I was intrigued by this idea of being distracted and being misled by symbolism. Later, I asked Juan Luis for his perspective on this.

"Most symbolism that we have now is the symbology that our ancestors have passed on as knowledge," Juan Luis explained. "Our ancestors were really effective at gaining an understanding of the meaning behind symbols because they got their information by channeling it from its highest source. Now we use their teachings as a reference for how we can use the symbols in our lives.

"But symbols can be distracting, too," he said. "In the world of symbols and forms, you can easily get lost in forms and formalities. When our ancestors left the knowledge of the symbols, it was not for us to 'know' about them, but so that we could connect with the essence. In your practice, in your path, you should go towards the essence. You should aim towards the spirit. Your focus is to connect with the Absolute, with the whole. When you are focused on the spirit of it, or the essence of it, or what you are calling the 'Actual,' then you don't even need the symbols anymore because you can connect directly to the essence of it. Because, why have a stone, when you can talk with the mountain itself? If the mountain gives you something of itself for your *mesa*—for example, a stone—then be grateful, because through the stone you can connect to the mountain. And, yet, the love and the essence of the mountain are already with you, regardless, so don't get distracted."

"What happens if you get distracted?"

"You'll be distracted! What is it that you are looking for, the forms or the essence? Which would you choose? What is your mission on your spiritual journey or on your spiritual path? It is to arrive at a connection with the whole, with the Absolute—that which we know as God, as love, or however you want to name it. If you go to a church and you pray in the way you were taught, you are entering into the formalities of how you should talk with God. And you don't actually talk with God, because you are just in the formality of it. It would be different if you just talked to God directly. When you are with the Medicine, for example, you enter into an absolute connection with the whole. You don't need symbology. You won't get lost in the formalities."

During the previous year that I had spent at home, sorting through my field notes, it had become apparent that my research participants were predominantly male. When I returned to Peru, one of my first requests of Amado was to help me find more women to talk with.

He brought me to see Mama Elena.

Mama Elena was a medicine woman—one of the few female shamans in the area. She was known for her healings, but perhaps even more so for her coca leaf divinations. One afternoon we arrived at her house, a sparse adobe structure with little furniture other than a table and a long case in which she displayed a variety of perfumed waters and other ingredients that she used in healings and *despacho* offerings. Doña Elena was a small woman with a beautiful round face and long black braids down her back. She squinted often, as if in need of glasses. Her age was difficult to determine, though Amado later told me that he guessed her to be in her late 60s. When we arrived, she was running late, as the evening before she had been called out to deliver a baby, and then, that morning, a client had unexpectedly come to her for a healing. Before she could see us, she had to finish preparing his remedy. When she finally sat down, she gave me a long assessing look. With Amado translating from her mix of Spanish and Quechua, I asked her how she became a healer.

"It all began in dreamtime," she began. "In my dreams these beings contacted me and told me, 'You must recognize who you are and you must walk this path.' This was when I was 25. But first I was struck by lightning when I was seven. And then I was struck again when I was 13. Then when I was 35, another lightening struck me again. There was reminder after reminder and still I didn't listen."

"What has your experience been as a woman in this profession?" I asked.

"It was a very difficult path to walk," she answered. "Many people didn't want to accept me in the community, or even in the family. They were, like, 'No, it's impossible. You can't be a healer. You must be a *bruja.*'"

"They thought you were a witch? Why did they feel that way?"

"I didn't have the right training. Everything was coming to me in dreamtime when I needed it. I didn't know all the names of the *apus,* I didn't know all the medicine plants, I didn't know lots of things. I was going to give up, and then I met a man who fell in love with me. And I told him, 'Okay, but I am not a regular woman. I am walking this path.' And he took me to this community where there were only the best healers who knew about everything and anything. I couldn't go there by myself; I could only go with a husband or a partner. Never just alone. I went there and that's where they told me about my path and how difficult it had been and everything. They told me that when I went back everything would change and everything would be different. And then they made a ceremony for me from 4:00 in the afternoon to the next sunrise. Everybody there introduced themselves to me as if they were mountains. They would tell me, 'I'm Apu Ausangate. If you come to me I will give you a *mesa*. I will teach you about what's happening in your community, how you can help them, what you can do for healing them and everything.' Or, 'I'm Apu Salkantay, and I can teach you this.' It was strange for me. I wondered why these people were pretending to be mountains. Even the children would speak like that. I was in a very untrusting space until someone told me that this was a very special village of healers and that when you receive the *mesa*, you don't become you anymore; you become the mountain. So, they take the name of the mountain.

"Finally, after my training was complete, they sent me home and told me that I needed to practice everything I had learned. 'This is your new life,' they said. 'To be a healer.' They said I needed to help people but that I could not charge anyone for six months. But in that six months that I was not supposed to charge, somebody offered me something in return for a healing. Because I was in so much need and didn't have anything else, I accepted it. My teachers found out and gave me another three years before they would give me the last secrets. And in those three years I was to continue to work without receiving anything back."

"Were you accepted after that?"

"My conflict has been with the men in that they do not allow me to be who I am. The first man against my path was my husband. Once I learned the art of healing, I got confidence. People were coming to me, recommending me to one another, and so on. But my husband was telling me, 'You must leave all this.' It was a constant fight. When I had a client to see, my oldest child would wait for me two or three blocks away from the house with all the medicine. I would tell my husband that I was going to the market to sell something, when actually I was going to do healing work somewhere. I did all my healing work in hiding from my husband. But then my husband discovered it and he got clever and said, 'Okay, I accept what you do. But you must take me.' He went with me, but his main purpose was to embarrass me. After the person was healed he would tell the person, 'Actually, my wife doesn't know anything. She's very bad at this.' People would become confused. So, then I no longer took him."

"Would you say that it is harder for a woman to walk this path, then?"

"For a woman on this path there is more suffering because we are limited to a certain space, while men on this path travel farther," she said. "They go farther. They are called to far places. They can leave their family and that is acceptable. But a woman cannot leave her family. So you have to be strong and you have to be brave."

When I asked her if there were other medicine women like herself, she replied, "More and more now."

"Do male healers and female healers engage with this work in the same way?" I asked her. "Or are there differences?"

"We work in the same way, but what a woman can do, most men can't do," she said. "That's what the men are afraid of."

"Why do you mean by that?"

"We work with the favor of Mother Earth. Men also work with the favor of Mother Earth, but, as women, we are in greater connection with Her than men. Men can't access that same energy. That's why women healers are very powerful and why men are afraid of them."

Someone called out from the other room. Mama Elena stood up.

"And now it is lunchtime," she said.

After lunch, she asked me if I would like a coca leaf reading. She instructed me to grab a handful of coca leaves with both hands, blow on them three times, and then release them onto a woven cloth on the table in front of us.

"How do you read the leaves?" I asked her.

Peering at the leaves, she mumbled something and waved her hand at me. I looked at Amado.

"She says you'll have the experience; you don't need the theory," Amado said, and then whispered, "She just describes things according to what calls her attention in the pattern. The way she does a reading changes all the time. It is always evolving."

Mama Elena was studying the leaves closely.

"You have a lot of headaches," she told me definitively. "You need to take care of your head and stomach. There is a lot of potential. There are a lot of possibilities, but you are not completely giving to those possibilities and to those potentials."

"Meaning?"

"There are some limitations in that area. Maybe something that needs to be changed energetically in your life and that is what is affecting your head and your stomach. Any doctor who would check you would not find anything. Because there is nothing wrong. But any healer that sees you will know that there is something that needs to be done."

She pointed at the leaves and said something that was mostly in Quechua.

"She sees a line of leaves that calls her attention," Amado explained. "That for her represents your journey."

"Your journey is long," Mama Elena said. "You are searching for big things. Huge things. But whenever you find it, there is still something missing. In this journey, it might be that you do not find whatever you are searching for. So you are not completely satisfied ever."

She picked out a couple of leaves and repositioned them within the arrangement.

"But now it will take only a little more searching and finding and you will be complete," she said.

She picked up a handful of the leaves and tossed them up in the air, repeating my name as she did so. When they landed again on the cloth, she leaned over and squinted at them.

"There is somebody who must be your partner or somebody who is really aware of how you are and wants to support you always," Mama Elena said. "It's a person who is always looking after how you are and what you are doing, but he's always too shy to walk the path with you. You are there in your journey and he is supporting you. He supports you a lot. This person doesn't know how to do all these offerings and ceremonies yet but soon he will learn."

She peered into the leaves again and made a little grunting sound.

"And," she added, "you must always listen to him."

"Oh yeah?" I asked, smiling a little. "Always?"

"Maybe just listen," Amado said with a wink.

Mama Elena was shaking her head sadly.

"And you keep telling Pachamama, 'There are no men for me.' You keep denying him."

"Uh-oh. Really?" I looked into the leaves to try to see what she was seeing.

"In order to fulfill all your wishes you need to completely accept him and invite him into your life," she informed me.

"And it will be so?"

"Yes."

With this, Mama Elena reached into the leaves once more and again seemed to be rearranging them—placing one leaf here, another one next to it.

"What is she doing?" I asked Amado.

Amado conferred with Mama Elena for a moment, and then said, "She says that the person she saw with you is someone who does not open his heart too much, but she just added a leaf and now he can open his heart more. So she just changed that energy."

"Do you mean that she's not just reading what is happening, but she can shift the dynamics of it, too?" I said, surprised.

"Oh yeah," he said. "She is shifting and manipulating energy, for sure. It is almost like, right from this table, right from this very place, you can be responsible for what is happening in the universe."

"Wow. So . . . let me make sure I understand this . . . first she reads what exists in the present, and she shifts what she doesn't like?"

"More or less. Not so much what she doesn't like, but she shifts those energies that aren't in balance."

"How does she do that?"

"Through adding a *yanantin* to it. Whatever is in existence will always have its complement. That's why don Ignacio was saying that there's nothing contradictory to it. If Mama Elena sees something out of balance— something that is too much one thing or another—she puts a *yanantin* to it to balance out the energy. To keep it from staying too much one thing or the other."

Mama Elena shifted the position of another leaf.

"Ah, yes! This is what she does," said Amado. "Look, now she is adding a *yanantin* to you. For you, your complementary energy is a person who doesn't work too much in the head. Because you are always thinking. To tell you not to think is like telling a fish not to swim!"

"But do you mean that that *yanantin* is another person, someone who will come into my life, or . . ."

"No, no. Not another person. Another version of you. The *yanantin* energy that she put down for you is another version of Hillary, but one that doesn't think so much. She sees a leaf that represents you and then puts another leaf with it. It's as if she was putting another Hillary in there, but one that doesn't work too much up here."

Amado tapped the side of his head.

"Okay, I think I get it," I said. "It's not that she is balancing me out with a partner or another person who is different, but rather she's balancing me out with another version of me."

"Right. She balanced you out. And when she saw that your partner did not have his heart open, she added a leaf to represent his *yanantin* and changed him to a person who has his heart completely open. That's how cool it is. That's why we say we don't believe in miracles, we count on them!"

"Do you have any questions?" Mama Elena asked.

"I'm interested in the idea of *yanantin*. How you suggest that someone could work with those energies. In their life, I mean."

"*Yanantin*, for us, is basically left and right, male and female," she said, sweeping the scattered coca leaves back into the plastic bag out of which they had come. "The way to work with *yanantin* is . . ." She paused for a moment and then shrugged. "It doesn't matter what you do. Everything you do, no matter what it is, it must have its *yanantin*. That way you are putting an extra force to that which you are already working on or perceiving. Whatever you perceive has to have a *yanantin*."

"The cool thing is that anything you perceive already has a *yanantin*," Amado said.

"Everything is in a pair, right from the beginning," Mama Elena interjected.

"I like that," I said. "I'm not sure I completely get it, but I like it."

A few days later, Amado, Juan Luis, and I took the train to Aguas Calientes, the busy tourist town that sits at the base of the Inca ruins at Machu Picchu. Before coming to Peru, I had asked Amado if we could make a trip to Apu Yanantin, the mountain peak that, appropriately enough, bore the name of my research topic. It seemed appropriate, even necessary, to make a journey to pay respect to what had come to feel like a kind of Mecca for me. I had asked Amado if we could make a trek to the base of Apu Yanantin and perhaps even climb it partway up. Amado told me that it could be done but only with great difficulty and effort, as there were no direct roads or trails to take us there. He and Juan Luis suggested instead that we do a day hike up to the top of Apu Putucusi, one of the mountains that shares space on the same mountain range as Apu Yanantin.

"In sacred symbolism, being at the top of Putucusi represents being at the top of Yanantin," Amado told me.

"Putucusi is a magic mountain," Juan Luis added, with obvious reverence. "We will drink the Medicine up there and it will show you what Putucusi really is."

And so it was decided. The three of us started up the trail midmorning. While a relatively short climb (the ascent taking no more than an hour and a half), it turned out to be one of the most grueling hikes I have ever done. The climb was entirely vertical, with a seemingly endless spiral of rock stairs as well as several wooden ladders that had somehow been attached to the side of the mountain, one of which was approximately 120 feet straight up. Each time we came to a ladder, Amado assured me that it was the last one. Each time we came to yet one more, I would curse at him for lying to me.

"But I wanted to make you happy!" Amado said, with a mischievous glint in his eye. "And you must have wanted to believe me, no? Remember, Princesa, your pain is my love."

"Bite me," I growled, and Amado and Juan Luis howled with laughter.

"Listen," I said. "I love you both. You know I do. But when we get to the top I am going to kick both your butts down the other side."

This just made them laugh harder, and the two of them dashed up ahead of me. Halfway up we stopped at a flat area and Juan Luis opened ceremony there, giving each of us half a cup of San Pedro to drink. Then we began to climb again. Finally, we reached the top.

"Gaaaaawd," I said, doubling over and resting my forehead on a boulder. "Okay, which one of you bozos is carrying me down?"

Amado tapped me on the shoulder and pointed behind me.

"There it is. Apu Yanantin."

I stood up and turned around.

"What do you think?" he asked.

It was beautiful. Perhaps it was partly because of the increased oxygen flow to my brain due to the strenuous hike; perhaps the little bit of San Pedro that I had taken was starting to kick in, giving everything a heightened quality; or perhaps it was just because the mountain held such a symbolic intensity for me on a deeply emotional level. Whatever the case, yes, she was absolutely beautiful.

I said just that to Amado, and then, catching what I had said, asked, "Is it a she?"

"Apu Yanantin can be a he or a she. That's why it is *yanantin*."

It was raining lightly, and the clouds floated across the landscape in front of us. As I turned to look, the clouds parted just enough to reveal the peak of Apu Yanantin off in the distance in front of us.

"She's got a double point," I said. "Not one peak, but two."

"Yes, Yanantin is almost like two mountains in one," Amado said. "It is about the essence, the double essence."

From where we stood, we had a condor's-eye view of the ruins at Machu Picchu across the valley below us. The gray stone of the buildings stood out against the deep lush green of the jungle foliage that contained it. Juan Luis brought me another half cup of the San Pedro. After I drank it, Amado suggested that I take some time to sit and connect with Apu Yanantin. He and Juan Luis went over to a nearby rock ledge and lay down. For the next half hour, I sat silently, staring at Yanantin and letting random thoughts wander through my mind. Eventually, the San Pedro began to take effect, though only moderately so. I felt a sweet sense of expandedness—nothing overwhelming, just enough so that my mind felt sharper, as if I had just woken up from a really good nap. I centered my attention on this idea of "symbolic" versus "Actual"—what the distinction was if there was one, how the two connected up, and how I could understand something that seemed to go beyond ordinary understanding. Staring at Yanantin, I asked for help in understanding these things.

I heard movement behind me and turned to find Amado standing next to me.

"Hey there," I said.

"How is your connection to Apu Yanantin, Princesa?" he asked me.

"Very nice," I said.

"Good."

"Is there anything I can do to deepen the connection?" I asked him.

"Yes," Amado said. "Smile."

And so I did.

An hour or so later, Amado and Juan Luis were perched on the tip of their rock chatting. I was entertaining myself by taking a look at some of the plant life growing around me. My eyes kept coming back to some beautiful ferns that, like most ferns, consisted of large fronds, each one made up of several smaller fronds that were an exact replica of the larger one. I was filled with the sensation—like a nudge or a tickle in the brain—that there was something important about the ferns that I needed to pay attention to. Some part of me was trying to remember something, but what exactly? I didn't know, but I was left with that same frustrated feeling of when you have a word stuck on the tip of your tongue, or when you have an itch that is just out of reach. I had the feeling that there was some connection between the ferns and my question about the symbolic versus the Actual. But what?

I began to free associate. Eventually, I started thinking about a *Nova* special that I had seen just a few months earlier. The program captivated me the moment I had landed on it. The show was titled "Hunting the Hidden Dimension," and it was all about fractals. Rather than endless chaos, fractal geometry theorizes that nature is made up of a series of repetitions called "self-similarity." If one zooms in to view a system from a microscopic perspective, it looks exactly the same as it does from a macroscopic perspective. Zoom in or zoom out—always the same. The pattern continues on and on. All of nature reflects this in one way or another, the show implied. From plants to weather systems to mountain ranges to the rhythms of the heart, fractals are speculated to be the basis for the very essences of life. The fern was noted as one of the most common examples of fractal geometry and this idea of self-similarity. The pattern of a fern repeats. Each frond is an exact copy of the larger frond out of which it grows (Schwarz & Jersey, 2008).

Fractals. This nudge that I was feeling . . . it had something to do with fractals. As I stood looking at the clump of ferns across from me, an image began to take shape next to it. It was so strange—almost as if an image had formed inside my mind and then had projected itself outward to become a three-dimensional image in front of me. It began as a shimmer and then gradually grew stronger and clearer until it was as though I were viewing a hologram.

A scene began to unfold in front of me. An old teacher and his apprentice stood next to the fern. The teacher pointed to one of the smaller fronds growing out of the fern.

"Is that the fern?" he asked his student.

The student hesitated, as if sensing this was a trick question.

"It's *part* of the fern," he said, finally.

"Yes, indeed. But is it the fern?" the teacher repeated.

The student said, his brow furrowed, "Well, no. It's not the fern."

"No," the teacher said, clearly pleased with this response. "It's not the fern. And, yet, without it, the fern would not be the fern either. It is this way that symbols work as well. Do you understand?"

"I do!" the student exclaimed, a smile of grateful understanding breaking over his face.

And so did I. The student's understanding was my own. The image in front of me dissolved and I was left with this insight: As the smaller frond is to the larger frond, so is the relationship of "symbolic" and "Actual." While the small frond is not the fern, nor is it not *not* the fern. It is not *It*, but it is part of *It*—which, perhaps paradoxically, makes it *It*, for it is an integral part of what makes up the greater whole. As with all fractals, the smaller part is reflective of the whole even though it is not the whole itself.

In the same way, it occurred to me, a symbol is not equivalent to the Actual. But it *is* a part of it, and, therefore, just as the fern would not be the fern without the totality of the smaller versions of itself that make it up, without the symbol, the Actual would not be the Actual either.

Not It, but also not not *It.*

Not It, but part *of It.*

It. *Because it makes up the whole.*

"Oh!" I exclaimed and crawled across the rock over to where Amado and Juan Luis were sitting. I told them about the image that I had seen and the insight that it had given me.

"The little part of the fern is like the symbol, right? It's all just a fractal, isn't it? A symbol is a fractal of the Actual. A symbol makes the Actual manageable to us. The *mesa* tool 'works' because the essence of the Actual is reflected and re-created within it."

Amado and Juan Luis were nodding. "Yes, Princesa! Continue!"

"So, then," I said, getting even more excited at the connections being made, "getting distracted by a symbol is kind of like focusing on the little frond and thinking that that is *It*. Thinking that you have connected to the whole when really it is only a little part of it."

I was on a roll.

"However," I continued, "even if you do get distracted by the smaller frond, or the symbol, that's okay because you are still seeing the totality of the whole through a glimpse at the microcosmic version of it. Since it is a fractal of it, and therefore reflective of it, then you have seen it. So, it can be a distraction from the rest of the plant, but, at the same time, it's not entirely a distraction because it is an exact reflection of the actual thing."

I looked at them both.

"Am I getting this right?"

"Totally!" Amado said.

"Exactly," Juan Luis replied, nodding. "The leaf is always part of the plant. The symbol is always part of the Actual. God is like the fern. We are part of the fern also. We are connected in that sense. Always connected to the whole through connecting to its parts."

"I get it," I said. "Or I get *something*. Something that works for me, at least."

I wandered back to my rock to think this over some more. A few moments later, Amado appeared with a crown that he had made out of the ferns.

"This is your prize for seeing the truth about symbols," he said, placing it gently on my head.

It was getting late and so we said our final good-byes to the mountain before heading back down.

"Thank you for bringing me here," I said to Amado and Juan Luis. "It was everything you said it would be."

"It was not up to us," Juan Luis said. "You were brought here and we followed you. You had programmed yourself to go to Apu Yanantin, and the mountain heard you. Our belief is that once you actually make it here, it is not that you came here but rather that the mountain brought you. The mountain brought you here because it wanted to share a powerful essence with you."

It had taken us an hour and a half to get up, but only half an hour to get down.

FIGURE 11: © Carl A. Hyatt, 2000, Wife and Husband, Ausangate, Peru

CHAPTER NINE

Male and Female

⟨⟩

As Jung (1953/1968) said of man and woman, "This primordial pair of opposites symbolizes every conceivable pair of opposites that may occur; hot and cold, light and dark, north and south, dry and damp, good and bad, conscious and unconscious" (p. 152). And so it is. Perhaps no duality has garnered as much attention, either in the Andes or anywhere around the world, as the dyad of male and female.

In the Andean perspective, male and female is considered the most fundamental polarity—the absolute basis of the philosophical ideal of *yanantin*. Scholars (Harrison, 1989; Platt, 1986; Silverblatt, 1987; Urton, 1981) have noted that indigenous Andeans interpret the world around them as if it were divided into two interdependent spheres of gender, that the polarities of male and female act as "the prisms through which the universe and society are viewed" (Silverblatt, 1987, p. 212). Platt (1986) was told by his Macha informants, "*Tukuy ima qhariwarmi*": "Everything is man-and-woman" (p. 241). He noted that when drinks are served, the Macha pour a few drops on the ground, speaking the name of the receiving divinity. This is done twice, which is explained as being *yanantin*, or "for the conjugal pair" (p. 245). Urton (1981) described at length how the people of Misminay, Peru, split the natural world into male and female categories. For example, natural phenomena such as lightning and thunder are considered either male or female, depending on the specific form that they take. Likewise, during our conversation, Dr. Jorge Flores Ochoa pointed out that the Q'ero people of the high Andes divide native animal species into categories of male and female. For example, llamas as a general category are considered male, while alpacas are considered female. Interestingly, however, these distinctions have not been applied to cows and sheep and other post-Conquest animals. Classen (1993) suggested that the division of the human body into male and female elements (left side female, right side male) reflects the Andean desire for achieving a balance between the genders. This equal division of energies within one entity is also revealed in the Inca and pre-Inca imagining of the creator deity Viracocha. While referred to as a "god," scholars (Andrien, 2001; Classen 1993; Cruz, 2007; Harrison, 1989; Joralemon & Sharon, 1993) noted that Viracocha is typically depicted as having both male and female attributes, implying that, as the creator of the world, the deity encompasses, integrates, and transcends all polarities. Similarly, other Andean deities come in pairs. Pachamama (Mother Earth) is typically matched with Inti Tayta (Father Sun) and so on.

In her study of Inca and pre-Inca society, Silverblatt (1987) noted that, based on this dual conception of the world, Andean men and women were seen as having equal status. Marriage, she noted, was celebrated as the formation of a unity made up of two equals. Although some tasks were defined as appropriate to men and others to women, women's work and men's work were seen as complementing one another, with each being equally necessary to the well-being of the household and community. Silverblatt, as well as others (Joralemon & Sharon, 1993), have pointed out that it was only after the Spanish Conquest that the once complementary gender roles were replaced with patriarchal relations and values associated with machismo. However, it has been noted (Allen, 1988, 2002; Harris, 1986; Heckman, 2003; Isbell, 1977; Platt, 1986; Seibold, 1992) that male-female symmetry still plays an essential role in both the social and ideological organization of the *ayllu* structure in many of the rural communities of the highland Andes. For example, the earth's fertility is considered strengthened by the combination of men and women working together (Heckman, 2003). The survival of the community is therefore seen as dependent upon the balanced union of the conjugal pair (Harris, 1986).

Scholars (Harrison, 1989; Platt, 1986; Vasquez, 1998) have observed that whether something is paired or unpaired is an important distinction within the Andean cosmovision. Harrison (1989) noted, "Quechua speakers persistently distinguish objects which are not well matched or 'equal'" (p. 49). Among the Macha, *yanantin* contrasts with *chhulla*, which refers to something that is unequal or odd—"one of things which should be twice" (Platt, 1986, p. 245). Vasquez (1998) found that the people of Cajamarca say that something incomplete is *chuya* [alternate spelling], meaning "the one who is missing its other" and that "in order to be whole, one has to pair up" (p. 100).

When I told Amado about the shocked response that my anthropologist friend gets when she tells the Q'ero that she has no husband or partner, he laughed and said, "They must say, 'How do you handle everything?' It's a big surprise, because, for them, without that partnership, life would not be possible."

"Why not?" I asked.

"They would say that unpartnered people are missing an important part of them. They say that when you don't have a partner, you are only half of a being. Alone, you are precious, you are unique, but you are only *part*. You are not whole yet. This is because when you are by yourself, you are either accumulating so much that it is overwhelming or you are draining yourself so much that you become weak. Because of that, you will feel fear or confused or lost."

Amado continued, "We believe that partnership is very important because, as they say, you may know yourself, but you can never *see* yourself. For that you need another person. You need other eyes, another perspective to see that. When you are a child, you have your parents, but when you become older you no longer have your parents to see you, to recognize you. As an adult, your *yanantin*, your partner, is the person who is there to see what you don't see in yourself, just as you are there to see in that person what he doesn't see in himself. That is why it is easier to take care of another person than of yourself—because you are not supposed to take care of yourself! For that, there is the other person. There is *ayni*. It's a service of love.

"It's a very powerful process," Amado said. "That's why they say in the communities that if you don't have a partner, you can't handle life. That's why they get surprised. Because given the ways they live, one cannot handle life in the community without a partner. Only when a person is paired can they truly serve the community. That's why the communities don't see you as the whole until you are together. I was in Chincheros the other day and I was telling all the single boys, 'You are only half men!'"

"It's pretty common in the United States for men and women to be unpartnered," I said.

"Yes. Communities in the North are made for you to be able to live alone. They kind of make it easy to do, but it is not completely possible."

Isbell (1978) and Allen (1988) have likewise reported that within indigenous Andean communities an individual is not considered an adult or a member of the community until marriage. Isbell (1978) wrote, "Persons are not complete until they have been joined to 'their other half,' their spouse in matrimony" (p. 23). Allen (1988) noted, "Cosmos, community, household and individual are felt to attain existence through the fusion of opposites like the *warmi* [woman] and *qhari* [man], each of which contains the other" (p. 208).

While the duality of male and female is perhaps the most fundamental polarity there is—not only for indigenous Andeans but for most of us walking around on the planet—for many of us it also feels like one of the most *challenging* sets of opposites to bring into complementary harmony. Among same-sex couples as well, one could argue that there is a continual dance of male and female energies that reside within each of us regardless of gender.

Given the importance that is placed on maintaining male-female equilibrium in the Andes—and given my own personal frustration experienced within this context in my own life—I was especially intrigued to hear what Amado and Juan Luis had to say about finding complementarity between male-female energies. One day I made a somewhat, though not entirely, tongue-in-cheek comment that it sometimes felt that the universe was playing a cruel joke to make men and women so different.

"Would you like them to be the same?" Amado asked, turning to look at me with surprise.

It was January 20, 2009—Inauguration Day in the United States. Across Peru there were celebrations that, on this day, Barack Obama would be made president of the United States. The extent to which this event had galvanized this area of the world was remarkable. In Lima, dozens of *curanderos* gathered for Obama's inauguration, stomping their feet, dancing, shaking rattles, blowing smoke, and chanting the new president's name while throwing flower petals and coca leaves at his photograph (ABC News, 2009). The four of us were in Uncle Ernesto's car, driving south out of Cuzco toward Puno, to an area called Cañón del Tinajani. There, Amado and Juan Luis told me, I would receive the final teaching that I needed to complete my work with *yanantin*.

Amado shook his head at my remark.

"In the Andes, we don't see the differences between men and women, Princesa. The differences don't exist, at least not in the way that you are speaking of. We don't focus on the differences. We focus on the qualities that only those two people can have together. Those qualities are what create the *masintin* action of the *yanantin* pair. As soon as you start to value that, you start creating harmony for you and your partner."

"That's definitely a better way to look at it," I said. "In the North, there is so much antagonism between men and women."

"Yes, that's why here in the communities that idea is taught. Because that is where the challenges are as a *yanantin* pair. Two beings in partnership always have to go through challenges, through tests, and the belief is that if they can make it through the challenges with ease, with harmony, and with joy, then they can be of better service. After going through those tests they can be much more powerful in whatever mission they have for the family, the community, or the world. That's why we have the tradition of the three levels of *tupay, tinkuy,* and *taqe*. Those three levels represent a process that unites you with God, with the soul, with *yanantin*."

"We talked about those three stages before," I said, "but in a more general sense of how they apply to self-other relationships. Now, I guess I'm wondering how specifically that works with romantic partnership. Can you tell me about them again in that context?"

Amado nodded. "The progression is *tupay, tinkuy,* and *taqe*. *Tupay* is the moment when the souls first meet. It is precious and sweet and powerful. Before, and in the communities today, *tupay* lasted for a year. Or two years. *At least.* Just the *tupay* level. But these days a lot of people fall in love as soon as they meet and they say, 'Yes! We are together forever!' And then they get married.

"But then, of course, they have to get through the *tinkuy* level. That's the dance. That's the lovemaking and that's the fighting. It's the action. The *masintin*. That is where the challenges are for the partners. Traditionally, the *tinkuy* level would last about five years. Sometimes in *tinkuy* there are children, even though still you are not married yet."

"Because in the communities marriage is not so much about the children as it is about the union between the couple, right?"

"Totally. It's all about the union part."

"For us, the kids tend to be the culmination of the union," I told Amado. "Or at least that is where the emphasis often is."

"A lot of children happen in the *tinkuy* level. After all, the *tinkuy* is how babies get made!" He laughed. "Many times in the *tinkuy* level one partner grows tired and doesn't want to continue—maybe because it is too hard. In our humanity, it is so easy to give up. And so they divorce. Because of that, in the communities you do not marry until you arrive to the *taqe* level.

"Some couples only go to the first level, to *tupay*. Even if they stay together for their entire lives, they do not arrive to the *tinkuy*. Some arrive to *tinkuy* and stay on that second level for their whole life. But in very special cases, and with a lot of support of the Masters, a couple will arrive to the third level, which is *taqe*. The *taqe* level represents absolute strength—for the family, for the community, and definitely for the planet. In our tradition, the *taqe* level involves figuring out how you share what you have created together. A lot of couples feel that they have arrived at the *taqe* level, but they really haven't because there is always one partner who wants to be in control. If there is a winner or a loser, then you are still in that *tinkuy* mentality, right? There is still that competition. Only when partners come into absolute cooperation, do they reach the *taqe* level. *Taqe*, you would think, is the level where every *yanantin* pair wants to arrive to, right? Actually, that is where they *have to arrive to in order to really begin*. *Taqe* is the beginning because it is about the mission that the two people have together. It is not only to grow together, not only to harmonize their energies together, but also to support the healing of the family, the community, and Pachamama. That's why any *yanantin* partnership has to go through these levels."

"How do you know when you've arrived at each level?" I wanted to know.

"The community is looking. The elders are deciding."

"There's that awareness?"

"Oh, yeah."

I laughed. "I'm sure my love life would be much easier and more successful if I had someone telling me what to do."

"They don't tell you what to do," Amado corrected me. "They are just witnesses. They are the ones holding the energy for you when you can no longer hold it for yourself. Because when you are in it, there is no way of being able to see it. The couple never sees anything. They are going through a process, and so the elders hold that essence for them."

"I remember when we talked about this before, you told me that, in the communities, teenagers are aware and consciously acknowledging these three stages.'"

"Yes, we are taught from a young age how to work positively with these energies."

"Of course," he said with a smirk, "then at some point you forget it all. On purpose. And that is when the elders are there to hold it for you."

A wave of regret rushed through me—regret at what might have been if I had been aware of these stages earlier in my life.

"I have to say that I am envious of that," I said. "I really feel that that is something that is missing—I would even go so far as to say *pathologically* missing—in my own culture. We are given no conscious training in how to deal with one another. We are rarely taught how to acknowledge the differences in male and female natures in a way that is respectful and understanding toward one another."

Amado nodded. "Yes, I have seen this."

"So, tell me, how exactly do they teach you this?"

"Women have specific teachings about men, and men have specific teachings about women. For a man, we are taught to understand a woman's existence in the same ways that we are taught to understand Mother Earth."

I gave him a questioning look.

"As you know," he said, "the word *pacha* means both time and space. For us, women represent the quality of space in *pacha*. A woman holds her essence like space. A woman is like Mother Earth—unchanging."

He gestured out the window at the scenery flying by.

"Look! This Pachamama isn't going to change for hundreds of years. This valley, those mountains there aren't going to change for many thousands of years. Men, on the other hand—we represent the quality of time in *pacha*. Men are like time, changing by the second, so young girls are taught that a man is something that you can never take for granted because, as he represents the time aspect of *pacha*, he is changing moment to moment. See? That's why men expect women to process things very, very quickly emotionally like we do. For us, while in one moment there might be some upsetness or something, in the next moment there will be complete forgiveness. Or love, or joy, or whatever. But a woman holds her emotions longer. Usually, a man will have a hard time with that because he's already changed that emotion very quickly, whereas women can't change it just like that."

He snapped his fingers. "For a woman, something major has to happen to shift that emotion. So, there is always that conflict. That's why we men are taught to respect Pachamama's process, because while our process is ever changing and shifts very quickly, like time, she is like space and remains steady. We train men not to be too fast with their decisions, and we train the women to be very patient and not to take anything for granted from a man because he can change all of a sudden.

"At their highest level, that is what these teachings really have to say— that you should never take your partner for granted," Amado said. "You cannot say, 'We will always be together.' Because that would be taking it for granted. And if you really love someone, you've got to liberate them. That must be one of the *most* important laws in the *yanantin-masintin* process— that you can never take for granted that you will always be together. That's the beginning of the sacred progression. That's what needs to be acknowledged the most."

He slapped Juan Luis on the shoulder. Juan Luis jumped slightly and turned around in the front passenger seat to look at us.

"For example," Amado said, "let's say I am the wife and he is my husband."

Juan Luis snorted and shook his head.

"What? Do you want to be the wife?" Amado asked him with feigned surprise. "No, no, I am the wife. Definitely."

He turned back to me.

"So, if I am the wife, I am not to take my husband for granted. Ever. I can't become too attached to him because, like time, he is always changing."

He narrowed his eyes at Juan Luis.

"But I will never divorce you!"

"Why are there problems in relationships?" Juan Luis asked. "Because a man gets married and starts getting fat like my brother here."

"Did you just call me 'fat'"? Amado asked. "It doesn't matter. I don't care what you say to me. I will never divorce you!"

"Okay, okay," I said. "I know you guys are kidding—or I think so, anyway," I said with a wink. "But that brings up a good question. Does all this just count for male-female relationships, or does it apply to men and men and women and women in love?"

"Yes, it applies absolutely," Juan Luis said. "In *yanantin-masintin*, it all counts. Gender doesn't matter." He paused and smiled. "Except between Amado and Juan Luis. In that case, one of us would have to be a woman!"

We all laughed.

"Men and women, women and women, men and men . . . a partnership happens because the cosmos has willed it," Juan Luis said. "At that point, humanity's way of thinking about things does not matter."

"So," Amado continued, "as I was saying, the first thing in a *yanantin* relationship is to never take for granted your partner. If you really love, you liberate. But why would you take your *yanantin* for granted anyway? Why would you even have to think about attachments when this love is already at the soul level and therefore is already eternal?"

"What do you mean, 'at the soul level'?" I asked.

"When I got married, Grandfather said to me, 'You're not marrying the other person, you are marrying the soul.' You have to love the soul, you know? Because in a few years this person might leave the physical body. When you get attached to the person, what you are creating is hurt and pain for yourself. That is why you need to liberate the person and love them at the soul level. In the Andes, that is what we call *winyi wayna*, which means 'filling eternally with youth to the beings you love.'"

"And when you use the word 'soul' you mean . . . ?"

"The soul is the essence. It is the essence that is God manifesting through a person."

"So, in order to love someone at the soul level you have to release them on the physical level?"

"Yes, because when you liberate them, there is sort of like a reciprocal energy in the cosmos that continues bringing them back. I'm thinking about how much I love my wife. Our connection is at the soul level. So, the first thing I need to do is liberate her. Not necessarily to let her go, because she is not really leaving, but to acknowledge that at this point in the connection that she and I have together, even if she were to journey a different

path without me, we would never be separate. That's the thing. It doesn't matter what path is taken; you and your *yanantin* are never separate. Even if I were to take another path for some reason, what is important for her to know is that no matter what happens, no matter what paths we take, we are never going to be separate again. That is the soul-level connection that exists."

"That could be a hard one for us Westerners to really get," I said. "To really embrace. We don't really think in soul terms. First and last tends to be the physical and emotional manifestation of a person.

"Why is that so difficult to really get?" I said, almost to myself.

"It's very hard," Amado said, nodding. "Even for us. This is something we are told as children, but then later on we forget and no longer put much attention to that soul-level connection. Everything in modern society points to the physical person—in fashion, in what we are taught about how a person should be in order to be the perfect man or perfect woman. But all these other things are just temporary and superficial layers of who we are. We become so distracted and so disconnected from that soul connection that we only focus on the person. And when that happens, you miss so much. That is something that we have to unlearn."

"There are levels throughout," Juan Luis interjected. "When you are in love often it is the human aspect of it that happens first. And then it becomes the animal aspect of it, where it is just instinct and everything from inside. And that becomes much more powerful than just the physical, sexual connection. Then it arrives to the cosmic level and that makes it much more powerful than just the animal. And then you come back to the human level again. When we are in love, we journey through different dimensions of that love."

"But that's it!" Amado exclaimed, suddenly getting animated. "That's it! Nobody can tell you how to love. To love is an ability we have come here with. Everybody. Even the person who has completely closed his heart because of whatever reason and cannot accept love can in a minute love like nobody ever did. It's our nature. All those different dimensions are a part of who we are. When love happens, it happens at that soul level whether you know it or not. It is almost at a point where it is not your choice, because of the way that the cosmos has woven us together. So, in practice, many of us, maybe even *all* of us, are already loving at the soul level. We just don't know it or acknowledge it in that way."

"But when you acknowledge it that way, it goes to an even deeper level," Juan Luis said. "The other thing that we are taught is that your *yanantin*, your love, is not just suddenly going to be born. Somewhere he or she is alive right now. He already exists. It's not like he or she is going to exist one day. Your *yanantin* is already here. The soul is already here, in preparation for you as you are in preparation for him. That person is also on a journey, in a preparation to arrive to that level of absolute purity and essence. Just like you. So, you never live life as if he is yet to arrive. He is always here and will always be here. Maybe you cannot connect with him physically just yet, or maybe you are already connected physically, but what you should start connecting with is the soul. Start with a soul-level relationship."

"That is why it is called *soul* mate," Amado said. "Even if your *yanantin* is not with you in physical form, you should, whenever you can, share some of your essence with him. Wake up in the morning and kiss the air and say, '*Amorcito, tú besito.*' Or when you are eating a sandwich you should say, 'Mmmmm . . . have a bite of this, my love.' Because then you are connecting to the soul."

"The love of your life is already in your own life, even while you are searching for him," Juan Luis said. "From the moment you are born into this human body, you walk this path with your *yanantin* already. It's not like it's going to maybe happen or maybe not. You already have a *yanantin*, right from the beginning."

"What you are saying reminds me of my favorite line from my favorite Rumi poem," I said. "It goes: 'Lovers don't finally meet somewhere; they're in each other all along'" (Barks, 1995, p. 106).

"So," I said, "does all this imply that our *yanantin* is just one specific person?"

"No, no," Amado said. "This soul can manifest through many people according to the different part of your life or where you are on your path. And that's the beautiful part of it. I have had my *yanantin* manifest with Grandfather, with Juan Luis here, with my father at one point, with my great-grandmother, my grandmother also . . ."

"Friends, family are all part of your complement, your *yanantin*," Juan Luis interjected. "Amado and I are your complements right now. You are such a strong and wonderful woman that you need two complements!"

"I like that!" I said.

"And you can be ours, too," Amado said. "And that is okay, because even though my wife is my *yanantin*, that *yanantin* energy can manifest through another person as well. Should I say, 'No thank you, I already I have a wife; I already have a woman?' No! All those connections with the soul are to be respected. They can't be taken for granted. That doesn't mean that when the soul manifests through another woman that you are supposed to marry her. No. With some *yanantins*, you are only to work together, not live together. In the community, they respect that, especially the elders. They would see this *yanantin* relationship happening and they would say, 'What is the work that you have together?' Obviously, it is not in partnership, as either one of you might already have a husband or a wife. But maybe there is something that you need to do together. Some service in the community."

"And neither is your *yanantin* always a *person*," Juan Luis emphasized. "It's like when we talk about the relationship of elements. The earth, the air, the water, the fire—they are not opposites. They are complementary always. And the communion that they have together is perfect. You are the manifestation of an energy, and your complement is an energy that is around you. That essence is *yanantin*. Not the person. An essence."

"That essence is the most powerful force," Amado said. "It doesn't wait for your will. Can you prepare yourself for love? No! It's too powerful. Nobody can tell you when, how, who. It's a force that, when the cosmos wills it, will flow and create new life. That's why it is the most powerful force on our planet."

"And also one of the most painful," I said with a sigh, thinking back on some of my own experiences.

"Sure," said Amado. "The *yanantin* part, that connection, is beautiful, is great, is cool. But the *masintin* part, the working through those three levels—that is a process. It hurts. It is human. It's not so easy or so wonderful at times. It is cruel, it is crude . . . everything.

"But," he said, with a smile, "without it . . . what kind of life would this be?"

I was about to agree with him, when Uncle Ernesto interrupted us. "*Estámos aquí*," he announced, pulling the car over. I looked out the window and my jaw dropped. I had been so focused on our conversation that I had not been paying attention when Uncle Ernesto pulled off the main road and onto the long dirt passage crossing the seemingly endless Altiplano.

Long ago, at the end of the Pleistocene epoch, the entirety of the high plateau of southern Peru was covered by a vast lake, the remnants of which are now known as Lake Titicaca, the highest navigable lake in the world. What remained when the lake dried out was an eerie landscape of stone monoliths formed out of volcanic red sand and sedimentation which had, over the years, been carved by the elements into a forest of strange rock formations. Some of these formations were impossible shapes that seemed to defy the laws of physics—top-heavy spires that looked as though they were only barely held up by the skinny pedestals supporting them. Others dipped and curved at odd angles. Many of these other chunks of rock had eroded to take zoomorphic shapes: a chipmunk the size of an elephant here, a 50-foot bird over there. Strangest of all were the humanoid forms—figures that had seemingly been frozen in time as they went about their various errands. Next to us, a 100-foot man carried a sack over his back. Up on a hill, an old woman hitched up her enormous skirt as if stepping over a puddle. Colossal faces peered at us from all across the cliffs.

We were insects in a garden of giants.

"Wow," I said, looking around. And then, because I could think of nothing else to describe what I was seeing, I said it again. "Wow."

"Totally," Amado said with a knowing smile. "Welcome to Tinajani, Princesa. Are you ready for your final teaching?"

"Christ, I hope so," I said and stepped out of the car.

FIGURE 12: © Carl A. Hyatt, 2004, Tinajani, Peru

CHAPTER TEN

Perfection Versus Wholeness

"Earlier, we were talking about the three levels," Amado said, appearing next to me.

This was not a question, but I answered him anyway.

"Yes," I responded, uncertainly. "*Tupay, tinkuy,* and *taqe.*"

We were walking down a dirt road—which was barely a road at all but more a place where the grass grew reluctantly. It stretched out across the high plateau in front of us, endlessly stretching into the horizon. The four of us—Amado, Juan Luis, Uncle Ernesto, and I—were barefoot. About half a mile earlier, we had come to a wide river that required us to wade across in order to pick the road up again on the other side. None of us had put our shoes back on after that, even though the ground was strewn with sharp pebbles that forced us to walk daintily. At an altitude of almost 13,000 feet, the air was cool, almost cold, but pleasantly so. Little curls of steam spun out of our mouths as we spoke.

"That's right," Amado said. "What I want to tell you now is that there is also a fourth level."

"A fourth?"

"Yes," he said. "It is known as *trujiy*."

"*Trujiy*," I said, trying out the word on my tongue a couple times. Amado nodded when I finally got it right.

"Why didn't you mention it when we were talking about this before?"

"Usually, we don't talk about *trujiy*. It's something that we know very well in the communities, but, like *yanantin*, we often don't access its full meaning. But I think it is time to now, no? Juan Luis prepared the Medicine for today for the teaching of *trujiy*."

After arriving at Tinajani, Amado, Juan Luis, and I had begun ceremony next to the car, each one of us drinking a cup of San Pedro before spending some time sitting on the side of the cliffs, connecting with the energies of the place.

"Out of respect we don't enter into the most important part of the temple right away," Juan Luis had told me. Later, we would go to a very special area of Tinajani. There, Amado said, "You will download what the sacredness of *yanantin-masintin* means."

After spending some time up in the cliffs, we had started the three-mile walk to the area of the canyon where we now were.

"Okay, so, what is *trujiy*?" I asked Amado.

"The *trujiy* level is very, very powerful," he said. "All the stages are powerful, but *trujiy* . . ." His voice trailed off. "You arrive at the *trujiy* level when you have completed everything and you and your *yanantin* have become a oneness. Because once you reach the *taqe* level, you are no longer two people, but one. *Trujiy* is then the point at which your *yanantin* departs or when you depart from your *yanantin*."

"*Trujiy* is the separation of the *yanantin* pair?"

"Yes."

"That sounds kind of sad," I said, not sure I liked where this was going.

"No! It's not sad at all," Amado said. "Because that separation is only the start of another, much higher level of union. *Trujiy* represents the capacity to be yourself again once you have experienced that *yanantin* union. After that, you become one single person again. But in that singleness you are no longer just yourself. You are One—with the *yanantin*, with God, with the essence. No matter what happens, you are One with all of that. Always."

Amado gestured to the landscape around us.

"This place is very special. We brought you here because it is a very powerful and very sacred place. Many Masters are reflected through the images carved in the mountains. In these mountains is stored all the ancestral knowledge of the Andes. For those of us who work in the spiritual realms, Tinajani represents the Akashic Records of Mother Earth. Because of that, our ancestors chose this place to be an ancient cemetery where they could store like seeds the very special people, the Trujiys, who were buried here."

"The Trujiys?"

"You see," Amado said, "agriculturally speaking, the *trujiy* is the best seed. The one that you can take to any land, any altitude, and it will produce the best fruits. If you ask anyone what *trujiy* means in Quechua, it is 'the best of the best.' The people known as Trujiys were thought of as the best seeds because they were the best of the best of the best at whatever they did. These were people who had arrived to their utmost level of evolution. And we are talking about both genders—not just men, but also women. These people had worked more than 100% with their *yanantin* and completed all three levels to become the best of the best of the best. Some were the highest spiritual leaders. Others were the most fierce and respected warriors. These people were leaders in their life for whatever gift they had brought to Pachamama, to their families, and to their communities. A Trujiy was a person who was always looked for. *Needed.* People all the way from the north in Ecuador to the south in Chile would come looking for this specific person who was a Trujiy, the person who had all the secrets, all the knowledge, all the experience, all the power."

He pointed to a long wall of rock.

"It was in this canyon that the Trujiys were buried. They were brought here so that when they left their physical temple they would be with the Masters eternally. And when they died, the whole community would pray together for more of these Trujiys to come back."

"And do they 'come back'?" I asked. "Are there Trujiys today?"

"Yes," Amado said. "In fact, it is beautiful that on the very day that we are here in Tinajani, January 20, 2009, the new U.S. president is entering." He nodded solemnly. "Because . . . Barack Obama . . . he is a Trujiy."

"Do you think so?" I asked, surprised.

"Oh, yes."

"How so?"

"Trujiys are leaders. Trujiys bring about change. Always."

Amado raised his hand and waved at a young man who was watching over his flock of sheep as they grazed in the grass. The young man waved back. The sheep, even with their mouths full of grass, continued to bleat, with an occasional low, guttural interjection by the ram. Juan Luis and Uncle Ernesto had slowly been catching up with us as Amado and I talked, and they were now walking with us.

"Yes," Amado said, "Barack Obama is a Trujiy."

I thought about this and then shrugged.

"Could be," I said. "I guess time will tell."

But Amado was insistent.

"He is! How could he not be? To already have moved so much in the world, so much emotion, and to have called forth the energy of millions of people around the world in this way . . . that is a Trujiy. I myself have the wish to return to the United States again now that Bush isn't there. Before I wouldn't go up there, but now I have that enthusiasm again. With Obama, there is the promise of a shift, of some kind of change. We are ready for that now. That is what we need. Because more and more, there is a lonely pilgrim in the North. The Eagle is becoming a lonely pilgrim."

"A 'lonely pilgrim'?"

"A lonely pilgrim," Amado repeated, nodding. "This is why knowing that each of us has a *yanantin* is so very important. Because while each of us might have so much will, so much enthusiasm, so much strength to do something that we know needs to be done, we can still feel alone. We can so often feel like, 'I can't do anything.' That is what has happened, not only in the United States but everywhere in the whole planet. That's why our ancestors always looked for a *yanantin*. It was a force direct from the Source that was there for you and with you so that you could do the service that you need to do in life. When you are touching the essence of *yanantin*, no longer do you feel incapable, because you always will know that there is that extra support for you in whatever your mission is."

"And that, Princesa," he said, stopping suddenly and pointing up ahead of us, "is why we brought you here to this place."

I followed the trajectory of Amado's finger to the enormous rock sculpture ahead of us. Like several of the other formations at Tinajani, it was an almost impossible shape. Its short, squat base seemed hardly able to support the rest of the monolith, which grew fatter and with more protrusions the higher it went. With Amado helping me "see" by pointing out the various knobs and divots, the sculpture began to take on the undeniable shape of a man and woman standing side by side, facing opposite directions, conjoined by a serpent that coiled around them.

"When man and the woman have come to absolute harmony, they become *trujiy*," Amado explained.

"Each one of us is *trujiy*," said Juan Luis, standing next to me. He pointed at the formation. "We call it *illawi*." He conferred with Amado for a moment about how to translate the Quechua word. And then he said, "It means something like 'cosmic weaving,'" he said.

"This is a powerful place," Juan Luis said, echoing Amado's words. "Mainly, we have come here because of this altar to *yanantin*, known as duality, or polarity, or eternal love. Here, you will connect to the sacredness of *yanantin*. What is important is to have great respect. To be aware. Your focus will change by the second here. In Tinajani, the Masters like to give you tests and challenges, so anything you might receive or perceive during the ceremony, please communicate it to us."

"Like what?" I wanted to know.

Juan Luis nodded thoughtfully. All at once he seemed far away, his eyes lost in the memory.

"Once I was here in Tinajani with don Ignacio, in ceremony with the Medicine," he said. "I closed my eyes and saw a man with a *chullo* and a poncho—like the people from the mountains. He was calling to me. 'Come, come! Let's go! Follow me! Follow me!' And I said, 'Where? Where are you taking me?' And the man, who I realized was one of the Masters, said, 'We have to go to play!' I was taken into a dark room where the only thing lit up was a table. The Master said, 'Do you want to play?' And I said, 'Master, what do you want me to play?' The Master brought a set of dice out of his medicine bag and showed them to me. Seeing this, I said to him, 'Please, Master, let me do something first.'

"I came out of the trance and went to don Ignacio. I told him, 'Teacher, there is a Master who wants me to play a game. What do I do?' And don Ignacio said to me, 'If he is a being of light, he will let you protect yourself.' So, I entered into the trance again, and said to the Master, 'Master, please, before we play I have to protect myself.' And the Master said, 'Okay, okay, but do it quickly! We need to play!' After I protected myself, the Master pulled out the dice again. And then I said, 'But what are we going to play for?' And the Master said, 'How about we play your luck?' Then I got scared. 'My luck?' I asked. 'Yes, your luck,' the Master said. 'If you win, you get this.' He showed me images of cars, a house, a big life, lots of money . . . very tempting stuff. Then I asked, 'But what if I lose?' The Master shrugged and said, 'If you lose, you just lose.'

"But then I looked around the table and saw a lot of people laying on the ground looking weak, sad, lost. I said, 'Master, who are they?' And the Master said, 'Well, they lost.' After this I was very nervous, because behind all these games, there is always a spirit eating up your luck. The Master said to me, 'Hurry! Hurry! Are you going to play or not?' I said to him, 'Master, I respect my luck too much to play with you.' The Master said, 'Are you sure?' And I said, 'Yes, Master.' And he said, 'Very good! Come here.' And then he taught me numerology, symbolism, sacred geometry, and how to read the dice—all the magic behind all these games. It was a great initiation.

"But it was also a dangerous test," he said, his eyes focusing on me again. "So, if, for example, you feel invited to do something or go somewhere, please communicate with us first so that we can help to guide you in this sacred place."

"Okay," I said.

"This ceremony that we are doing here is about entering into the best aspects of yourself, Princesa." Amado said. "Here, you will receive directly into your heart exactly what the Masters have been waiting for you to receive. Only some are chosen to come here. Our moments are chosen and they bring us this way, in ceremony. They bring us for very special reasons. So be ready. For anything."

"Okay," I said again. "But *am* I ready?"

"You are ready," Amado said, "but are you prepared?"

"Absolutely!" I said, hoping it was true.

Amado and Juan Luis both laughed and nodded approvingly.

"Yes! That's what we wanted to hear," Amado said.

They walked away and I was alone. I turned back to the rock figure in front of me—man and woman, conjoined for all eternity. I waited, hoping for something exciting to happen, some otherworldly experience like in Juan Luis's story. If this was to be my final teaching, I wanted it to be a good one, something that left even my experience of the stars moving/not moving and my vision about fractals and symbols in the dust. I wanted

Revelation, some final piece of the puzzle that would in an instant let me integrate *yanantin* wholly and completely. Then everything in my life would make sense forevermore.

As I sat there, I could feel the effects of the Medicine deepening. My senses began to wake up all the way, and then it was as if the world around me had just had an exclamation point added onto it. Everything seemed to have taken another dimension onto itself, as if even the most infinitesimal qualia that make up creation had chosen to reveal their true character. The blue and green tones hidden in the rusty red of the stone masses leapt out, competing for attention with the bright pinks hidden within the yellow green of the scrubby canyon grass—a grass that doubled its own sense of presence by rubbing its blades together, rustling in the wind like people softly whispering. Not to be outdone, the canyon walls vibrated against the wind with a long, low "huuuuuurrrruuuummm!"

But along with these calming sensations came unpleasant ones as well. The young man had moved his sheep closer, and, little by little, the sweet rustling of the grass and the low humming of the canyon walls was overtaken by the ugly cacophony of the high-pitched whining of the sheep, punctuated every now and then by the low, lunatic bleat of the ram. The sound bounced off the canyon walls and filled the air, amplifying it to a maddening pitch. I tried to block it out of my mind by focusing on the wind, on the *illawi* stone in front of me. When that did not work, I tried to embrace it as part of the landscape of which I was trying to be a part, rather than give in to the belief that this sound was getting in the way of whatever Revelation might be waiting for me. The sound was beyond irritating. I found myself growing physically nauseous.

And then, for whatever reason, just as I thought I might lose it altogether, all the sounds—the shrieking of the sheep, the whispering of the grass, and the humming of the canyon walls—all began to merge into one. And then, even that oneness disappeared and there was nothing but a frozen silence, a big emptiness, as if I had gone temporarily deaf.

Before I had time to be alarmed by this, some wheel within my consciousness began turning backward. It started slowly and then picked up speed, as if time itself were moving in reverse. If this were a movie, it would be at this point that all the action on the screen would stop, frozen in motion for two or three seconds, and then begin moving backward.

Flashes of memory from the last two years flooded my psyche.

Barack Obama . . . He is a Trujiy.
Men and women as time and space.
Ferns and fractals.
Trickster apus. Visions of life and death.
The Chavín faces. The Lanzón. (My god, the Lanzón!)
The stars moving and not moving. Schrödinger's Cat.
Self and other. Tinkuy battles. I think, therefore, I think it over.
The prophecy stone. The Eagle and the Condor.
Meeting Juan Luis for the first time in the plaza. Laughter. Followed by
more laughter.
Amado. Laughter and tears.
Stepping off the plane. Out of the airport and into that fugue state.
Beginnings.

Suddenly, in my mind, I was back to the place where I had started. Back again to that point at which it all began. It was then that I had the utterly joyful and, at the same time, absolutely horrifying realization that none of it really mattered. None of it. The struggles, all the searching, everything that I had experienced over the last two years meant nothing because, in the end, all it did was lead back to this deep, glorious, heart-wrenching silence. And in that silence, meaning was irrelevant. Whether there were shapes in the rock or were not shapes in the rock did not matter a bit. It is all the same, one way or another. If the stars are moving or not moving . . . who cared, when trying to figure that out was a ridiculous attempt? In that silence, I was relieved of the obsessive urging to make meaning, for there was no meaning to anything. And that flash of insight was both blissful and painful. I had never before understood the strangely addictive power of the *tinkuy*, of the ecstatic friction that results from the antagonism of the polarities grappling with one another. While we might hate the struggle, or love the struggle, what does one do when the struggle stops? A loop is created in our minds that catches us and will not let go. Or, rather, we will not let go.

In that nothingness, there was no choice but to cease trying to make meaning of anything. In that oiled-up condition of the psyche, the urge to struggle had nothing to grip onto, nothing to give it traction and impetus and *purpose*. In that space, everything just *was being*. If there was more to know, to learn, it did not matter because, for better and for worse, in the end there is just silence. And in that silence we can stop.

Just stop.

For the first time in years, I felt the mad urging for answers leave me. And while on the one hand that was a glorious release, a deep pain came with it as well. Was this what it all came to in the end? After all the years of research, of experience . . . was it really to end this way? Not with a glorious flash of Revelation that would make the world make sense but with just this dull silence? Some strange nothingness? A part of me tried to fight that nothingness, but in the end I had no choice but to give in to it. It was all I could do. I was tired. It had been a long two years. I took a drunken step forward and felt my legs buckle. I sat down, exhausted, onto the ground, my head falling into my hands.

Awhile later, cold rain began to fall. I opened my eyes and found Amado and Juan Luis standing over me.

"How's it going?" one of them asked.

"Er . . . 'kay. I guess," I said, blinking.

Juan Luis bent down and looked at me.

"You have *huachuma* eyes," he noted.

"*Huachuma* eyes," I repeated, brushing the dirt and grass that had stuck to the back of my pants as I stood up. The two guys regarded me with interest but said nothing. We walked silently back to the car.

It took me a while to feel ready to discuss what I had felt there, and, thankfully, Amado and Juan Luis did not press me to talk about it right away. A few days later, back in Cuzco, I discussed my experience in the canyon with Amado. I admitted that on some level I felt a little embarrassed that I had not had a grander vision, that I even felt some letdown about the experience.

"After hearing Juan Luis's story, I wanted some mind-blowing experience," I confessed. "A Big Revelation. But instead . . . it felt so quiet that it was almost disappointing."

"But that's the Revelation!" Amado exclaimed, throwing his arms open.

"What do you mean?"

"What you experienced. That silence . . . *that* is the essence of Tinajani. Other people have powerful revelations and visions and teachings and training and all of that, but only seldom do people get what you got, which is absolute silence. Absolute peace. Absolute harmony with everything that there is and everything that there isn't. That's very powerful. It puts your mind completely busy and at the same time completely blank. Because after Revelation there is a struggle, too. Not necessarily to understand or to receive, but to integrate it into your life. For Juan Luis, after that game with the Master, he was at peace with himself for about three or four days, but even now he is still processing it. But with what you got . . . that's exactly what *trujiy* is about. At that point, you go to a whole other dimension of experience. That's what so many people look for. And like you say, they find it in the very place that they began. It is at that point that the Trujiy, the pilgrim, arrives to inner peace, to inner absoluteness, and also to absolute nothingness. That's it! That is it. That which is almost disappointing—maybe because it *is* so simple—is exactly the essence that we can find in *trujiy*. At that point, there is just that natural flow of not thinking before you do. It's like thought can come still, but first there's that peace, that silence, that natural instinct to act, to serve, to do. In the process of the *tupay* and *tinkuy* and *taqe*, there's so much happening all the time. There's full actions; full dynamics. The level of *trujiy* is exactly what you experienced. It's just that pure silence, when one aligns with that absolute everything and absolute nothing. That's it. That's *trujiy*. Those are the cosmic seeds. At that point, you are more than ready. So, you have arrived to that."

I shook my head. "That's great to hear . . . sounds great, anyway . . . but realistically speaking, I know myself, and I know how hard it will be for me to hold on to that once I am back at home. How do I do that without the Medicine?"

"Listen, because this is important," Amado said. "There is no such thing as 'without the Medicine' anymore, Princesa. In fact, there never was such a thing as 'without the Medicine.' The same vibrations that we get with the Medicine were encoded in your DNA the moment you were conceived. What the Medicine does is turn on certain switches that were always there. The connections were always there. The installations were always there. Everything was there. Inside you. Even if you had never taken the Medicine, the process would have occurred. It's just that with the Medicine, the transformation happens faster. The switch was turned on the moment you started this journey, and more so now that you have physically taken the Medicine. And now that San Pedrito has begun this process of clearing blockages, it will continue not just for days but for *life*. Once you have been with San Pedrito, it is in you, *always*, even if you haven't physically taken it."

"I hope so," I said doubtfully. "It is so easy to lose connection to the experiences that I have here. Especially when I go back home. Last year was a hard one for me. For a lot of people. There has been so much loneliness and depression there for so many."

"While you were here, going through so much magic, also over there was happening so much magic," Amado said. "When you go back, you can't even imagine what will be waiting for you. This year, 2009, is about the completion of a difficult cycle. Now it is time for the next level, where you no longer need to feel loneliness or depression but rather where you can celebrate all the miracles that are coming into your life because of the journey that you took, because of the pilgrimage that you took to find yourself and your *yanantin*. This is a new year. A new life. New everything. So many things will happen in this year. Obama will be president, and that is going to bring change for the United States, and a change for the United States represents a change for the whole planet. Everything is in perfect timing for this material that you are writing about to enter, to give to the people there. That's my vision. It has to happen. The reason I showed that puma to you . . . the one on the prophecy stone . . . is that in you, Princesa, is the sleeping puma. When that puma wakes up, it will have the power to affect the world. Think about it! You could have very easily gone back to the United States after your first trip and said, 'Yeah it was fun. It was nice. I took a picture.' But you kept coming back, over and over again, entering deeper and deeper into your awakening. And still you know that there is yet so much more. What you have experienced is a seed about entering into the essence of *yanantin*. Ten years from now, you will be working with it with a whole different perspective because it will have evolved. But what you are doing now is necessary as a seed to give fruits and to grow. That is the importance of this. But this is just a beginning."

He sat up and leaned forward slightly. "For me, my perception is that the work you are doing is bringing another soul to this pilgrim as a strength, in order for this awakening to continue. You are bringing a *yanantin* to that pilgrim. You are bringing that soul mate to this path, to this mission, to this service. So, I am no longer only just one Amado, but now two. You are not just one Hillary, but now you are two. That is *yanantin*. That's why we no longer need to walk as lonely pilgrims. Not anymore. Now we have our *yanantin* to travel with us on the pilgrimage. And this pilgrimage is not to a place or to a specific direction. It's not to the *apus*. It's not to the *huacas*.

It is *into*. It is about us going deeper into ourselves. That is why I told you that the *pachacuti* that we are now facing is about a return of the essence, a return of that highly evolved soul. It is about meeting ourselves again. The other thing is that while you may be journeying *into* yourself, you don't journey *for* yourself. You journey for those who are not on the path. You do it for those people who are right now in this moment sitting in an office and have basically signed on a piece of paper to offer their whole life—or a big part of their life—to be in there. We journey for them. Those people in politics who are completely disconnected from our planet and only care about economics and power . . . we journey for them, too. In the pilgrimage, we never journey for ourselves. Instead, we journey for those who are not on the path. Because those people need a *yanantin*."

He sat back again. "I don't necessarily have hope in politicians," Amado said. "Rather, it is the people that we least think of in the North who have the power to bring this major change to the whole planet. To me, that is no longer a hope. That, to me, is almost a *promise*. It is as if the cosmos and the *apus* and Pachamama are all telling me, 'Amado, just breathe. You have your part to play. Keep your tail straight up. North Puma will wake up. Don't fear. Don't give up. Don't be tired.' The thing is, your work is bringing that awareness of and that connection to *yanantin* not only to the people in the North but also to the people here in the Andes. I will tell you something—until you came here with the interest in opening to it, I hadn't gone this deeply into *yanantin* since I was a kid. Because even though it's there, part of this culture, we don't necessarily put a lot of attention to it. It's easy to forget. It's easy to take it for granted. But then you and I started working on this project, and I was paying attention to it so much! So, for me and Juan Luis and many other young people, it is a reminder to keep our tails straight up and stay in that essence.

"I love it. I love all this work, Princesa. Will it be a book? Get it published for sure. It's very, very good. All the research, all the material you have here . . . I am telling you, it is juice for the thirsty. The story is beautiful. It is really inviting, and also there is some secret coding in it for those who can access it. At this point, it is no longer a message. You are giving a very powerful gift with this. It is amazing. It is important. Eventually, I can already see that if this work was published and people here also had access to that, they would be like, 'Wow! What have I been missing?' It should be taught in the universities here. It is the time when young people need to reconnect with that. And when that happens . . . how many miracles are waiting to greet us?"

He whistled through his teeth. "This is only the beginning," he said again.

"I love that you feel that way," I said. "Of course it makes me feel very good."

I laughed and shook my head, feeling self-conscious.

"I have to tell you, though," I confessed, "I've been trying to figure out what this idea of *yanantin* is all about for the past two years—longer, even— but even now I barely feel as though I understand a fraction of what it is all about. When I started this, I wanted to understand it perfectly. I had this image that by the end of this project I would have completely integrated this idea of *yanantin* into myself and then I would have everything figured out. Life would be perfect. *I* would be perfect.

"But," I said, shaking my head again, "I feel very, very far away from that."

That *had* been my mission all along, hadn't it? To find a way to resolve the opposites in a way that achieved some kind of permanent balanced perfection. Jung (1953/1956) once stated that both as a culture and as individuals we needed to learn to value wholeness rather than perfection. *Perfection*—that was the ultimate psychological legacy of the antagonism of the opposites in Western culture, wasn't it? It was splendid or savage, but not a mixture of both. Never a mixture of both. Not really. Some part of us was always fighting that coexistence.

I had once gotten into a conversation with Juan Luis about this idea of "perfection" versus "wholeness."

He said, "Once I heard a Master say that the person who has the most wisdom is the person who has fallen the most. The person who can teach us is the person who has fallen many times. Maybe—outside of this world, outside of this life, outside of this state of consciousness—perfection really exists. But inside of ourselves, where we live, we are always with our imperfections, our limitations, and our pains. This is imperfection, yes, but it is also perfection. Nothing is perfect or imperfect. It is just life and sometimes life is hard. Life is like sea waves. You cannot always be on top. It would be unreal to be on the top all the time. You would be spiritually stagnant. You wouldn't learn. You have to get to the bottom and get to the top again. In order to go higher, you have to go lower, and then go up again. A lot of people try to hold on to the high points, and in that moment they stop growing. They stagnate. If you do not hurt, you are not alive. The mistakes hurt, but the pain teaches you that you are alive. If it didn't hurt, you would be dead. You would not be alive, and what a sad situation it would be to live like the living dead."

I thought about this as I talked to Amado. "I know all that sounds pretty silly, and probably the antithesis of what I was supposed to learn from all this," I told him. "It's just that, even after all we have talked about and all I have experienced, I'm not really sure where I am with all this. How much I really understand. Tacitly, I mean. At a core level."

"I know it is very difficult, but this is the most important thing, for you and for everyone," Amado said, taking a breath. "It is not necessary to understand any of this, Princesa. *That* is the most important thing. With *yanantin*, just its presence is already affecting you, whether you are aware of it or not, just like your presence is affecting it. That's why *being* is the essence. *Being*. Not 'doing,' not 'vibrating,' not 'activating.' Not even doing ritual or ceremony is it. Because *being* is the ceremony. In every moment the *tupay* is constantly happening. The *tinkuy* is either being denied or accepted. Just so has the *taqe* already happened. *Already*. And now the *trujiy*. It doesn't matter where you are or what you do. Just your presence here represents *yanantin*. So 'understanding' it is not important. What is necessary is to be fluid in your life. Just to continue to live life. To continue down your path and not to worry. From here on, the only homework you have is to be happy. Some people say, 'How can we be happy in a world so terrible, with poverty, with starving children?' But for that we have the responsibility to be doubly happy—in order to bring balance to the planet. *Yanantin* is to be born, to be reborn, to live life, to experience, to enjoy, profoundly and intensely in constant gratitude. That is the essence of *yanantin*."

Two nights later, Amado, Juan Luis, and I got together for a celebratory dinner to mark the end of my fieldwork. We reminisced about the last two years. We clinked our wine glasses and wished each other good health. Juan Luis wanted to know if there would be any sex in my story. I told him, "Maybe in the sequel." And we laughed. The boys told me stories about some of their wilder, more off-color escapades. Amado stopped in the middle of the telling and with a sheepish look asked if I was going to use it in my study. "Maybe in the sequel," I said, and that set us off again. The people sitting at the next table got up and moved to the other side of the restaurant. We tried to behave—with varying degrees of success. The waiter brought our dinners. Juan Luis ordered another bottle of wine. An hour later, there were tearful good-byes and promises of future journeys together.

The next morning I flew to Lima, then back home.

Epilogue to the Narrative

―― ◉◉

I N *THE SUN ALSO RISES*, one of the characters asks another, "How did you go broke?" To which his friend replies, "Two ways. . . . Gradually and then suddenly" (Hemingway, 1926/1954, p. 141).

What makes this exchange funny, in a bittersweet kind of way, is that it reflects the reality that change can, and in fact usually *does*, occur two ways—gradually, without our consciously noticing it, and then all at once when we have the sudden realization that some aspect of our life has been transformed when we weren't paying attention (or even sometimes when we *were* paying attention). I give a similar answer to people who ask me how my fieldwork in Peru transformed me:

Little by little and then all at once.

I understand that what they are really asking is, "*In what ways* did your experience transform you?" but, even so, Hemingway's line still feels like the truest response I can give. So many of the inner shifts that occurred within me during my time in Peru happened, and are still happening, little by little, at the unconscious level, in ways I barely recognize. And yet, every now and then, I get a sudden jolt of recognition that a transformation has

occurred, that I am now responding to the world in a significantly different way than I did before I began this study. Oftentimes, this recognition
sneaks up on me and does feel instantaneous. So when people push me
further, wanting to know the specifics of the psychological shifts that I
underwent, I find myself stumbling somewhat.

There's no neat denouement to this story. No tidy resolution. In a more
"Western" literary model—which usually satisfies us with a beginning,
middle, and definitive end—the narrative would have closed with me having achieved some glorious Revelation, an *Aha!* moment that would have
resolved all my own psychological tensions once and for all, leaving me with
some grand insight into the human condition as a whole. It does not. Even
the final vision in Tinajani, which resulted in me "returning to the place
from which I started, and knowing the place for the first time" (Bateson,
1991, p. 307), was revelation with a small "r"—an important insight, for sure,
but not the final piece of the puzzle in an individual's search for complementarity. For *yanantin*. But this, I have come to realize, is exactly the
point. A human life, like the Andean vision of time, is a spiral. It is not a
fixed condition looking for its end, but rather a continuing creation and
recreation in every moment. As Amado said, "That's why in the Andes, we
don't have a creation story, because creation is happening constantly, every
day." This view—that life is being created and recreated every day and that
we must greet each moment on its own terms—may be the crux of the
Andean complementary worldview in its most idealized form.

As one of my colleagues observed after reading the final chapter of
the narrative, "The fact that you ended where you began makes complete sense. Your frame of mind and perspective was wholly different and
resembles the spiral that you discussed in your piece where you can come
back and tweak; you can come back and see where you were. It's not like
going backwards, but it gives you another go around at something and it
also speaks to the cycles of life, the ups and the downs that repeat like a
corkscrew. . . . It's almost like you talk about stars dancing—they move,
they don't move, they dance, they don't dance. Well, when you look at
your journey ending where you began, that's only one way of looking at
it. Because if you look at a spiral, you're not really exactly where you were
before, but you are in the same neighborhood. You are an orbit ring above
or an orbit ring beyond where you started. And, actually, that is a really
wonderful thing. It's like a merry-go-round but a tilted one. [It's a] familiar

perspective through a different filter, or through a filter that has had some subtle colors added to it."

The constant re-creation of the world in this spiral fashion is, I believe, why Amado's final message to me was that *being* is the essence. *Being*, not *doing*, for the doing invariably takes care of itself. On a personal note, I will say that today, almost two years after my final fieldwork trip, I still find myself with a greater sense of peace, a calmness that I had not felt before I began the study. For me, Amado's description of the four stages of relationship (*taqe, tinkuy, tupay,* and *trujiy*) was an opening into the creative potentials that emerge as a result of the tension of this dance of opposites. The tension is a blessing, not a curse. It is a force in itself, a wave that we ride into the next moment, the next opportunity. Looking at it through this lens, I have begun to understand what Amado meant when he said that the essence of *yanantin* is "just to continue to live life. To continue down your path and not to worry." The rest will take care of itself. Whether the world is splendid or savage, or whether I am splendid or savage, does not matter so much. These things now coexist in a way that they could not before. And it feels great.

FIGURE 13: © Carl A. Hyatt, 2005, Apu Ausangate

CONCLUSIONS

The Global and the Local:
Reflections on *Yanantin*

THUS ENDS THE PERSONAL NARRATIVE. Some who read an early version of the manuscript wondered if by comparing Western and Andean philosophical models in this way I was trying to make a political statement about the superiority of the latter over the former. Others wondered the same thing about my choice to use autoethnography as my method of inquiry, which, in some ways, rebels against the traditional ethnographic aim to keep researcher and participant in more or less separate psychological domains. One reader took issue with the inclusion of the aspects of the narrative that made reference to George W. Bush and Barack Obama. And then there were those who felt the narrative wasn't *enough* of a political statement; that I should include a discussion of what the subject matter and the methodology had to say about the greater context of postcolonial fieldwork, ethnographic interpretation, and its relevance to global interaction.

Was I trying to make a political statement with this work? Yes and no. On the "no" side, when I started this project what I really wanted to do was to satisfy my own scholarly interest about what *yanantin* means to the indigenous Andeans living in the region of Cuzco, Peru. As time went on, my focus then expanded to include a more personal challenge, to see if it was possible to make a shift in my own philosophical presumptions in order to integrate this complementary vision within my own, Western-based paradigms (which, it has been argued, tend to approach the polarities in a much more antagonistic way). Regarding my methodological choice, as noted in the introduction, it very quickly became apparent to me over the course of my research that the intersubjectivity of autoethnography was the best, if not only, way that I could illuminate those aspects of the phenomenon of Andean complementary dualism that had become important to me—that is, how this ideology is understood both by my Andean participants and by me as a cultural outsider. My method of inquiry was therefore driven by what would work best for the subject and situation, rather than by an intention to make a methodological statement.

I recognize that it would not be too much of a stretch for a reader to assume that I included Amado's statements regarding George W. Bush and Barack Obama in order to push a particular political perspective and agenda. One early reader of the manuscript felt that any and all discussion of U.S. politics and policies should be removed entirely, as it would be jolting to readers who had, by that time, settled comfortably into the timeless and spaceless quality of the narrative. From an aesthetic standpoint, I agree that the inclusion of these two political figures *is* somewhat jarring to the narrative flow. I also recognize that by including them I risk alienating readers who do not share the political perspectives that Amado was espousing. Had I been writing a work of fiction, I likely would not have included those details.

But this is not a work of fiction. It is intended to reflect the lived truths of a phenomenon to the best of my and my research participants' abilities to articulate them. It seemed to me that if I were to remove these aspects of my participant's perspective I would be committing several sins of qualitative research. First, as social scientists we make an ideological and ethical commitment to reveal lived truth to the best of our understanding. Therefore, any and all data that seem significant for illuminating the subject of study should be presented for the reader's consideration regardless of the researcher's—and, potentially, the readers'—personal biases. Given that, how dare I deny the reader the opportunity to consider all the data pertaining to this subject? Second, how dare I consider denying Amado the forum to express what he considered to be a significant truth regarding the

manifestation of *yanantin* in his lifetime? To do so would be both a practical and ethical violation of the aforementioned agreement of qualitative
inquiry. Finally, by removing aspects of the dialogue that I was somewhat
personally and aesthetically uncomfortable with, I would be disregarding
a primary premise held by many forms of qualitative inquiry: that personal and cultural knowledge is rooted in the historical and environmental
context in which one lives. Put another way, one's understanding of a phenomenon is circumstance-embedded and thus wedded to both local and
world events. In order to create a thorough picture of a phenomenon, the
researcher must consider the historical setting within which these interpretations take shape, both in the mind of the researcher and that of the
research participant. For the sake of methodological and ethical rigor, I
ask readers who take offense to the overtly political flavor of some of these
dialogues to remember that, personal values aside, one cannot deny the
influence of these two figures on the world stage, and therefore the influence that they have on the testimonials of individuals who are directly or
indirectly affected by their choices.

So, *no*—in that sense my intent was not to make this research narrative
political in the sense of being a "call to action" to overthrow the current
Western philosophical paradigms and research methodologies or a com-
mentary upon past or present political leadership. It was simply a personal
and intellectual endeavor, a matter of following my interests and using
what worked to get me there.

But, then again, I suppose I can't claim that my intent was *completely*
apolitical either. In the act of trying to change my own sense of beingness
in and with the world, I did find myself fighting—though Amado would
probably more rightly call it "engaging in a *tinkuy* with"—my culture of
origin and its particular psycho-philosophical stance. As I attempted to
understand and integrate the indigenous Andean philosophical model, I
became more and more conscious of the deep-seated assumptions inherent
in my own cultural mind-set. Because of this, the study became a highly
revealing exploration of the unconscious life of the Western mind (albeit
with a sample size of one—me). In doing so, I could not help but note the
ways in which the philosophical premises of my cultural upbringing limited my sense of ease and psychological freedom in the world.

Also on the "yes" side of the question of the political nature of this
piece: As a researcher specializing in the field of the anthropology of

consciousness, I do what I do in large part because I enjoy the process of deconstructing my own personal paradigms regarding what constitutes psycho-philosophical "Truth." I also enjoy providing opportunities for others to deconstruct their own presumptions as well. Though I don't necessarily agree with all elements of the movement, I guess I am a postmodernist at heart. I tend to mistrust grand narratives that imply that there is one universal "Truth" that fits all times, places, and circumstances. I believe that we are well served as psycho-philosophical beings when we break apart our "habits of mind" that keep us frozen in one perspective of the world and of ourselves, though this is always easier said than done.

This is probably why Andean complementary dualism holds such fascination for me. While acknowledging that it is both impossible and improper to draw an absolute parallel between the two, I would like to make the tentative observation that, in their most idealized forms, Andean complementary dualism and postmodernism mirror each other by sharing certain philosophical commitments. As a philosophical movement, postmodernism is a response to and rejection of the post-Enlightenment philosophy of modernism, which seeks to uncover and align itself with universal standards and/or laws that are constant over time and space. Modernists claim that the best epistemological system is based on certain a priori principles that are always and forevermore certain, rational, and unchanging. In this way, the modernists believe, the world can be "known" rationally. Postmodernists, on the other hand, focus their attention on revealing the illusory nature of these "meta-narratives," which, it is argued, do not reveal the true nature of the world and, as a result, smother individual spontaneity and freedom of choice. Similarly, in the Andean world reality is not regarded as a solid, self-contained given, but as a fluid, unfolding process, one that is continually shaped and reshaped by one's actions and beliefs, as well as the actions and beliefs of others. Through *ayni*, or the reciprocal exchange of energies, individual realities are mutually constructed and, thus, "shared."

As Juan Luis said in chapter 1,

What I can say is that what is real for me might not be real for another person. You would look at the people around you and know that each person is a cosmos. Each one has lived something different from the other. And what is most important is what each person has to teach. So why would we spend time finding out who has reasoning and who has not? What is real and what is not?

Or, as Amado reflected,

[E]verything you believe, everything you know, everything you experience, is not really yours. Nothing that you think is happening within you is actually yours. It could be real for the person who is next to you, who is witnessing it. This is how we share realities. That is why there is such a truth when Juan Luis says that what is real for you is not real for the other person. That is exactly so.

Similar to postmodernism, indigenous Andean philosophy stresses the importance of *experience* as the best means of revealing knowledge. Just as reality is ever changing and unfolding moment-to-moment, knowledge, too, is self-revising. Because of this, epistemological decisions cannot be made through a priori assumptions, but must be redetermined according to each new situation. In this way, world and self are transformed at the same time, unfolding in a dialectical dance.

One reader of the narrative made an interesting summation of the distinction between Western/modernist and Andean ways of knowing, saying, "The Western model feels like it's constructed out of one's head, whereas the Andean model seems much closer to observation of 'Where are we? What kind of system are we in? What are the laws of the natural system that we take our life from?' While you may get out of balance, you know where to look in order to get back in balance, whereas when you are in your head and you are running theories out, there is no limit to theories because you are in your head, until you bang up against reality. . . . What I keep thinking of is [your experience with] the fractal fern. Getting an 'Aha!' insight into the way in which all that works. That's an insight grounded in experience and self-revelation as opposed to a deduction of a deduction of a deduction. Yes, afterwards you then have to go check it out, see whether it's fantasy or not, but when you are working in the realms of '[I'm learning something from] my teacher's teacher's teacher's teacher who took a class from Nietzsche'—where's the original contact with reality? . . . On the one hand you have learning from learning and on the other you have learning from experience. That insight right there could transform your whole relationship to the rest of your life."

As noted, in the Andean world, to "know" reality is to establish an intimate relationship between oneself and the aspect of existence that one wants to understand. For my research participants there is both an implicit and an explicit understanding that knowledge involves a joining of essences between entities, and that this joining can be created or reinvigorated through various practices aimed at blurring I-Thou, self-other boundaries. By doing so, the two entities shape, inform, and empower one another through their interaction, which, my participants suggested, plays itself out in the four-stage process of *tupay* (the meeting), *tinkuy* (the engagement and unfolding), *taqe* (the merging), and *trujiy* (the separation and continuation). In this way, they say, "Creation is happening every day."

This comfort with creation and re-creation may be why, as argued in the introduction, the Andean world has been so successful at integrating the practices of outside cultures without losing the fundamental themes that constitute the foundation of their original philosophical perspective. It may also account for the Andean perspective on good and evil, which, much like postmodernism, tends to blur the boundaries between these moral concepts without sacrificing an ethical impulse.

"According to the beliefs of the Andean cosmovision, there is no such thing as good or bad," Amado told me. "Whatever is positive can be negative in a moment. Whatever is negative can be positive in a moment. . . . Everyone is interwoven with the cosmos in order to be who they are, even those people who are doing these rapes and murders. It is almost at a level where you have to support them, at least with a prayer."

As noted, this view does not mean that my participants hold a laissez-faire attitude toward acts that could be considered "evil." *Quite the contrary.* When I asked them whether they would choose to take action against something that they considered to be wrong or evil, Amado and Juan Luis were shocked that I would think otherwise.

"Of course!" Amado said. "If it is in our hands? Oh yeah! Yeah, yeah, *yeah.* No doubt. No thinking twice about it. But then, again, how do I know what's right or wrong? First, you have to know how to recognize it."

In a similar way, the postmodern approach to ethics does not abandon moral concerns but seeks to recognize them and then deal with them in novel and more thoughtful ways. The postmodernist belief that "morality is not universalizable" is not meant to imply that one should not make ethical claims. Rather, it is intended to offer an alternative to "heteronomous [*sic*], enforced-from-outside, ethical rules for the autonomous responsibility of the moral self" (Bauman, 1993, p. 12).

"[D]o not be mistaken," wrote Caputo. "Deconstruction offers no excuse not to act. . . . Undecidability does not detract from the urgency of decision; it simply underlines the difficulty" (1993, p. 4).

While the modernist perspective very often hacks the Gordian knot of morality in two, thus creating polarizations and absolutes such as "This is moral; that is immoral," both the postmodern and Andean perspectives recognize that nothing is that clean and simple. Both philosophies urge us to consider an issue from all sides before then slowly and carefully attempting to unravel it to gain some greater sense of clarity. It is not that we should cease taking stands ethically, these philosophical perspectives suggest, but rather that we need to be aware of the limitations of the human perspective and of the habitual constructs that become so engrained in us that we cease to be consciously aware of them. Instead of relying upon a standardized system of ethics, the individual must therefore make the effort to consider an issue anew in each moment before deciding which to be the correct, or most ethical, course of action to take. This sense of personal responsibility, it has been argued, makes the individual *more* moral, not less. As Bauman put it, "[U]ncertainty is bound to accompany the condition of the moral self forever. Indeed, one can recognize the moral self by its uncertainty" (p. 12).

A more in-depth analysis considering the similarities and differences between Andean and postmodernist positions would be interesting indeed. However, such an analysis is not what this final section is intended to achieve. I make this abbreviated comparison between Andean and postmodernist perspectives for two reasons. First of all, I do so in order to suggest that those of us who align ourselves and our work with the philosophical perspective of postmodernism (regardless of the exact *degree* to which we align ourselves with it) might do well to consider the ways in which the Andean world has adapted these same (or at least similar) epistemological premises to the "problems" of day-to-day living, which postmodernism often fails to address. While postmodernism as a philosophical/political stance is relatively new to the Western world, these same ideals are an ontological given for many of the Andeans who I interviewed for this study. In many ways, the "dream" of postmodernism is being lived in the

Andean world and therefore might provide us with clues for how to apply these premises to the microcosm of interpersonal relationships, the macrocosm of global interaction, and everything in between.

One reviewer of the original manuscript felt that, in particular, the *"yanantin* stone" and the corresponding prophesy regarding North Puma and South Puma described in chapter 3 was particularly relevant to the question of how these principles might be applied to cross-cultural relationships in general. As the study of global interaction is not my field of expertise, I will not presume to discuss this topic with any kind of authority. However, it is interesting to think about the possibilities, in particular how we might apply the four stages of *tupay, tinkuy, taqe,* and *trujiy* to all manner of interpersonal, intercultural relationships. Along those lines, I will offer for consideration the possibility that—not unlike Amado's description of the shifting roles of North and South Puma—at the same time that many Westerners continue this postmodern experiment, the Andean world is, in some areas, integrating more of the Western, modernist position. Perhaps this is an aspect of what the prophesy stone represents—the changing philosophical stances of the opposing yet complementary relationship of North and South America, Western and Andean ways of being, which Amado stated constitute a *yanantin* pair. Maybe yes, maybe no.

This consideration of what the indigenous Andean philosophical standpoint might offer us regarding global interaction leads into my second reason for making the comparison between postmodernism and Andean philosophy. I also make this comparison to underscore that the Andean beliefs and practices do indeed constitute a "philosophy." I feel the need to make this statement because it seems to me that there has been a general (though certainly not total) lack of acknowledgment among Western philosophical scholars that Latin American belief systems—and in particular *indigenous* Latin American belief systems—represent a philosophical model as sophisticated as any other we might encounter. An amazon.com book search using the phrase "Western philosophy" garnered 22,792 results; "Taoist philosophy" 2,402 results; "Hindu philosophy" 6,601 results; and "Buddhist philosophy" 7,862 results. In contrast, a search using the phrase "Latin American philosophy" revealed only 1,394 results and "indigenous philosophy" 425 results. Likewise, *The Dictionary of Philosophy and Religion* (Reese, 1996), while providing an overview of the major schools and thinkers of Eastern and Western thought, contains no entry for "Latin American" or "indigenous" philosophical models. While this is hardly an exhaustive meta-analysis, the results of this search do reflect reluctance (either conscious or unconscious) among scholars to include the indigenous systems of thought (Latin American or otherwise) under the designation of "philosophy." Perhaps this is because Western scholarly frameworks have tended to view indigenous beliefs and practices as "irrational," thus going against the Western belief that "true philosophic development requires conscious and formal inquiry . . . [leading to] the formulation of *rational* questions about the origin, the true nature, and the destiny of man and the universe" [emphasis added] (León-Portilla, 1963, pp. 3–4). Perhaps the continuously transforming and therefore seemingly ambiguous nature of indigenous Andean ideology and practices has created this misconception of its irrationality and lack of conscious development. Perhaps, too, the historical lack of a written language has prevented visibility—and therefore respectability—of the complexity and multifaceted nature of these worldviews.

This is unfortunate, for my research participants are indeed "lovers of knowledge" in every possible sense that that phrase is meant to convey. From what I observed during my fieldwork, the indigenous Andean worldview displays all the essential "-ologies" (epistemology, methodology, ontology, etiology, and so on) that one would equate with any highly evolved, highly complex, and highly rational philosophical system. Throughout the process of researching this topic, I was consistently surprised at the complexity and subtleties of the Andean worldview, which, like most things, becomes even more multifaceted the further one delves into it. Although my prefieldwork literature review took me part of the way to understanding this, I did not get a tacit sense of Andean complementary dualism as a living, breathing philosophical system until I stepped into it, both physically and emotionally, at the experiential level of engagement. Having done so, I now feel compelled to underscore the significance of Andean complementary dualism to the study of philosophy in all its cross-cultural forms. This brings us back to the consideration of global interaction, for the pursuit of *ayni*—knowledge of self and other through intimate relationship—demands that we truly "see" the other and, in doing so, give the other his or her due as an equal participant in the world's construction, both philosophically and otherwise.

So, okay, this work may have been *slightly* political after all. Or at least more political than I had (consciously) thought or intended when I first

began this study. But, really, can any researcher escape making a political statement in the process of collecting and interpreting his or her data?
Krippner and Winkler (1995) made the case that all research methods can
be viewed as inherently political, intertwined as they are with issues of
power and legitimacy. This is certainly true of ethnography, in which the
researcher must make choices—based on his or her own assumptions about
how knowledge is achieved and at what "price" it is acquired—about how
we will relate to the cultural "other" standing in front of us and how we will
attend to our own personal stories that threaten to cloud the "objectivity"
of our research.

Rabinow described ethnography as "the comprehension of self by the
detour of the comprehension of the other" (1977, p. 5). In the case of autoethnography, the opposite is also true. In this case, one attempts to compre-
hend the *other* by the detour of the comprehension of the *self.* The hope and
intent is that this über-reflexivity and über-transparency will allow for an
even deeper "mutually constructed ground of experience and understanding" (1977, p. 39) between researcher and participant, thus leading to greater
illumination of the phenomenon under study.

Have I achieved this goal within this work? Overall, I do feel that autoethnography was a good choice—perhaps the only choice—to get me where
I wanted and needed to go. As a method of inquiry, it led me to data and
corresponding insights that I would not have been able to get to had I stuck
with my original plan of conducting a more traditional ethnographic study.
To be clear, I have nothing against traditional ethnographies. Not at all.
Quite the opposite. I have absolute respect and admiration for the many
forms that ethnographic inquiry has taken and continues to take. But I also
believe in methodological diversity and that certain subject matters call for
a form of inquiry in which researcher and participant intentionally inhabit
the same plane of beingness in the world. By doing so, "truth" is illuminated from within the context of living, breathing human beings interacting with one another, engaging in a dialectic of intersecting narratives.

Over the course of this study, I certainly discovered that striking a
balance between the alternating roles of self and other is not at all easy.
In hindsight, I can see a number of limitations to what I have done here
in that regard, and a number of places that I would do things slightly differently the next time around. For example, rereading the narrative (and
even the beginning of this concluding chapter), I see that I have spent

much time discussing the contents of my own emotional experience that arose as the result of doing the study and very little considering how being involved in the research process affected my participants. Rabinow (1977) points out that within the research process, participants can often be pulled into a "liminal, self-conscious world between cultures" (p. 39), in which the research participants are forced to reexperience and reevaluate their life worlds, creating the potential for them to undergo their own psycho-spiritual deconstruction as a result of participating in the study.

In the case of my own work, one example of this comes at the very end of the narrative, when Amado says,

> I will tell you something—until you came here with the interest in opening to it, I hadn't gone this deeply into *yanantin* since I was a kid. Because even though it's there, part of this culture, we don't necessarily put a lot of attention to it. It's easy to forget. It's easy to take it for granted. But then you and I started working on this project, and I was paying attention to it so much!

For me, his reaction was a triumph of this method, for it signaled that, at least as far as Amado was concerned, being a participant in the research was more constructive than destructive to his psychological and cultural experience. Part of the reason I chose autoethnography as my method of inquiry was that it felt like a highly ethical methodology in that it forced me as the social scientist to turn the eye of observation *inward* onto myself, thus reducing the tendency to act as the all-knowing "expert" (which could lead to disempowerment of my cultural participants). But while my presence seemed to have a positive effect on his emotional and cultural well-being, Amado's acknowledgment of the impact of the study on his own life was a humbling reminder that no methodology is completely without risk of turning our participants' worlds upside down under our inquiring—even *self*-inquiring—gaze. In hindsight, I am sorry that I did not ask my participants for further feedback on their experience of the research process itself, for clearly I was not the only one who changed as a result of this study. While I did my ethnographic "duty" by following the currently prescribed institutional procedures for ethical research in the field, I do feel that I missed a step by not bringing this aspect of my participants' experience even more fully into the narrative. In my own defense, the study was primarily intended as an exploration of how my participants relate to the idea of *yanantin*, and therefore it was on this aspect of their experience that I kept my focus. Still, given that this research project also turned into an experiment in alternative methodologies, I now feel that the lack of attention to this aspect of my participants' experience leaves the narrative conspicuously one-sided.

As far as other limitations of this work go, there are certainly other aspects of the cultural phenomenon of *yanantin* I could have addressed, other directions in which I could have taken the study. There are other ways I could have utilized my research methodology in order to be more expansive in scope and more intellectually rigorous. However, despite its limitations, I do feel that my research and the resulting narrative offer something to individuals with a variety of academic and/or personal goals. My hope is that this study will add to the larger ongoing dialogue within Latin American studies, in particular that of complementary dualism as the basis of the Andean philosophical system. Additionally, researchers seeking alternative qualitative methodologies may also find that this work provides an opportunity for discussion regarding both its successes and its limitations in illuminating certain aspects of the human condition. And given its reflection upon how such transformations in consciousness take place within the human psyche, psychologists might consider how Andean models of consciousness can lead us to greater personal and social health. And so on.

Carl Jung (1953/1956) once pointed out that "[the opposites] ought, in their harmonious alteration, to give life a rhythm, but it seems to require a high degree of art to achieve such a rhythm" (p. 59).

A high degree of art to achieve such a rhythm. I like this idea and the possibilities that is suggests for the continuation of this topic. It causes me to ask: What "high art" inspired by Andean complementary dualism can we create for ourselves, both as scholars and as citizens, to help us move beyond the tension of the opposites in our daily life, whether they are the tensions within our own psyches or between individuals, groups, nations?

NOTES

Introduction

1. In the context of this book, I refer to "indigenous Andeans" as a way of distinguishing individuals who are directly descended from the original inhabitants of the region prior to the Spanish Conquest. Within this definition I have included individuals who are of mixed indigenous and European descent (often referred to as *mestizos*, meaning "mixed blood") who have aligned themselves with the pre-Conquest philosophies and practices. In this same way, when I make reference to the "indigenous Andean philosophical model," I am referring to the complementary dualism that has provided the basis for the region's social and spiritual practices prior to the Spanish Conquest.

2. The term *kuraq akulleq* refers to an individual who has achieved the highest ranking of *paqo* or shaman in the spiritual tradition of the high Andes.

3. "Andean" and "Andes" refer to the geographical region that extends through much of South America through Argentina, Bolivia, Chile, Colombia, Ecuador, Peru, and Venezuela. This area consists of various distinct groups. There is a general acceptance among scholars that the people of this region share enough of a common history, linguistic lineage, and ideological outlook as to constitute being categorized as a single culture-sharing group designated as "Andean" (Andrien, 2001; Astvaldsson, 2000; Barnes, 1992; Carpenter, 1992; Dover, 1992; Isbell, 1978; Mannheim, 1991; McDowell, 1992; Murra & Wachtel, 1986; Sherbondy, 1992; Silverblatt, 1987; Stone-Miller, 2002; Taussig, 1980; Urton, 1981). This categorization is considered particularly true of individuals living the traditional or pre-Conquest lifestyles of this region, who engage in what Dover (1992) described as

"a set of [philosophical] mechanisms which together engender a uniquely Andean perspective" (pp. 7–8).

4. Here I use the term *philosophical model* not in the strictest sense—that is, not to imply an intentionally created system of discursive thought and logic—but rather as a system of shared meanings (both conscious and unconscious) through which a culture comes to organize, understand, and refer to reality (Taylor, 2000). A philosophical model provides the basis for how members of a culture-sharing group relate to the world around them—for example, what moral codes inform their interactions with both human and nonhuman entities, what epistemological practices are considered valid forms of "knowing," the methods of attaining knowledge, and the ways in which such knowledge should be acted upon. Here I use *philosophical model* interchangeably with other terms such as *worldview* and *model of reality*.

5. A *dualism* refers to philosophical and/or spiritual systems in which existence is believed to consist of two equally real and essential substances (such as mind and matter) and/or categories (such as being and nonbeing, good and evil, subject and object). This study focuses on two particular kinds of dualism: (1) a "dualism of antithetical terms" (Ajaya, 1983, p. 15) in which the opposing categories are viewed as being entirely independent of one another and/or eternal enemies that relate only through their antagonism and opposition to one another, and (2) a "dualism of complementary terms" (Ajaya, 1983, p. 15) in which the underlying ontological belief is that everything has a counterpart without which it cannot exist, thus rendering the opposites interdependent parts of a harmonious whole.

6. It has been argued (Lévi-Strauss, 1963; Maybury-Lewis, 1989a; Needham, 1973) that all cultures across time and space identify and make meaning of the world through binary oppositions—dyads of complementary or opposed elements such as male/female, good/evil, spirit/flesh, sky/earth, and so on—constituting a "universal tendency to think in twos" (Needham, 1987, p. 229). Because of this, some maintain, every culture can be understood in terms of its relationship to the opposites. However, critics of "bipartization" (as noted in Needham, 1973) are wary of binary classification, arguing that sorting cultures and their ideologies into categories of twos is a false attempt to discern order in human experience. Some (Sawada & Caley, 1993; Beattie, 1968) have suggested that binary classifications do not arise naturally, but may be prefabricated by the anthropologist-as-observer in an attempt to create meaning and order out of disparate cultural traits. As Almagor (1989b) acknowledges, "It is possible to present almost any social phenomenon in any society as a dual formation, but that does not mean that society possesses a dual system or even a scheme of a dual classification" (pp. 20–21).

Reviewing the various arguments for and against the use of binary classifications provides the opportunity to become aware of myriad debates surrounding any attempt to organize a culture according to strict analytic forms. That said, the following study is based on the assumptions that (1) no matter what the ontogenesis of dualistic or binary thinking, no matter whether duality is truly the most accurate of all forms of categorization, human beings *do* have the tendency to organize their worlds into contrasting pairs of twos, making it a useful (albeit perhaps incomplete) organizing tool and that (2) given this "preoccupation with polarity" (Maybury-Lewis, 1989a, p. 6), much of human consciousness is devoted to trying to understand and mediate the relationship of the opposites, both on spiritual and social spheres.

7. In recent years, it has become commonplace to use the term *Western* as a way of signifying (1) cultures of European origin and (2) cultures that are not European in origin but that have been so strongly influenced by European immigration and/or globalization that they have adopted many of the religious (i.e., Judeo/Christian), philosophical (i.e., rationalistic/linear), economic (i.e., capitalistic/entrepreneurial), political (i.e., democratic/participatory), scientific (i.e., positivistic/materialistic), and various other social values that are historically distinguishing features of the European mind-set. Tarnas (1991) noted that the Western paradigm, both in its spiritual and secular realms, is marked by certain long-standing themes, including, (1) Reductionism, the belief that complex systems can be understood by reducing them to their individual parts; (2) Absolutism, the desire for concrete and unchanging "facts" about the world that can be proven universally true across all times and in all situations; (3) Objectivity, the belief that in order to understand the true nature of reality a separation must be placed between the subject and object, observer and the observed; and (4) Individualism, the emphasis on the pursuit of personal happiness and individual success rather than the individual's relationship to the society in which he or she lives.

8. There exists much debate about whether it is appropriate to use the words *shaman* and *shamanism* when describing the healers and ritual specialists of indigenous communities. Kehoe (2000) has argued that "'[s]hamans' and 'shamanism' are words used so loosely and naively, by anthropologists no less than the general public, that they convey confusion far more than knowledge" (p. 2). Although I personally do not take issue with the use of the words *shaman* and *shamanism* when referring to indigenous healers and ritual specialists in a cross-cultural context, I do agree that, when possible, it is appropriate, both ethically and academically, to refer to these individuals in the way that they and their communities refer to themselves. Therefore, within the context of this book, I have tried to limit the use of the words *shaman* and *shamanism* to instances when I am referring to indigenous healing practices and those individuals who, as Krippner (1992) put it, "are socially sanctioned practitioners who purport to voluntarily regulate their attention so as to access information not ordinarily available, using it to serve the needs of members of their community and the community as a whole" (p. 12). When discussing Andean shamanic practitioners specifically, I will either use local terms—for example, *paqo* for the shamans of the highland Andes, *curandero(a)* when referring to practitioners of the north coastal region, and/or whatever terminology the participants use to describe themselves. When discussing Andean shamanism as a whole, I will most often use the terms *shaman* and *shamanism* as a way of encompassing all terms and traditions.

9. For example, the introduction of money rather than reciprocal labor as the primary medium of exchange, and community economics that emphasize reciprocity and maintenance of social harmony have, in many areas, given way to the forces of the capitalist Western market (Glass-Coffin, 1991, 2004).

10. For a more in-depth discussion of the impact of the New Age movement on the city of Cuzco, Peru, see Hill, 2001.

11. In their study of the *curanderos* of north coastal Peru, Joralemon and Sharon (1993) noted that there is a seeming discrepancy as to which type of dualism provides the metaphysical basis for the shamans' rituals. In some instances a more *antithetical* form of dualism seems present. For example, some shamans describe the two furthermost "fields" of their *mesas* or altars as reflecting "the opposition between good and evil" (p. 5). Shamans who align themselves with Christian conceptions of good and evil often place ritual items associated with "evil" on the left side of the *mesa*, with curative, "positive" items placed on the right side. However, as Joralemon and Sharon (1993) noted, "many of the oppositions are Christian, but the manner in which they are handled is Andean" (p. 175). Despite this apparent antithetical, adversarial tone of the ritual as a confrontation between moral and immoral energies, they suggested that this opposition is done more in the spirit of harmonization than domination and is tempered with the belief that the so-called negative force with which the shaman enters into battle contains healing energy that is just as essential as the "positive" side. Rather than seeking to destroy the former in favor of the latter, the shaman learns to harness potentially destructive energies and channel their use for the greater good.

12. In the context of this study, I use the word *consciousness* in several different ways: (1) in accordance with the definition provided by Krippner (2002), who has used the term to refer to "an organism's pattern of perceptual, cognitive, and/or affective activity at a given point of time" (p. 8); (2) following Edelman's (1992) idea that consciousness arises from relationships between perception, concept formation, and memory; (3) following Josephson and Rubik's (1992) suggestion that consciousness consists of experience and reflection on experience, allowing the individual to create meaning about his or her situation as well as that of others; (4) referring to the subjective realm of human psychological experience through which thoughts, sensations, perceptions, emotions, and an awareness of self, other, and the world are processed; and, finally, (5) regarding its role within the mind/body debate, as a transcendent, spiritual essence that exists independent of the physical body.

13. One of the main premises of this study is that the philosophical model within which an individual is raised has significant influences on his or her personal psychology. By *psychology* I mean to describe the way in which the individual makes meaning of the world, either consciously or unconsciously, and which in turn shapes his or her attitudes and behavior toward self and other (Ajaya, 1983). In the context of this study I use the word to imply a focus on how adopting a philosophy of complementary dualism initiates transitions in the development of identity, personality, character, and selfhood in an individual brought up in a model of antithetical dualism. I have kept the use of this word to a minimum when discussing my Andean participants. This is because while the Andean people have most certainly developed systems of thought and action for assisting the individual in dealing with the mental-emotional complexities of the human experience, the cultural framework in which this takes place is so different

from that of the West that it feels misleading to use the term *psychology* in this context. This is particularly true given that many of the current forms of Western psychology ignore or deny "spirit" and even "mind." Indigenous Andean healing practices, on the other hand, do not place these aspects of the human condition in separate domains but instead see them as interrelated (Apffel-Marglin, 1998). Therefore, mental-emotional health cannot be addressed without at the same time attending to all other aspects of the individual. Knowing this, it felt important to keep the use of the word *psychology* at a minimum when discussing the inner lives of my Andean participants.

Chapter One

1. With two exceptions, all the participant names used within the book are pseudonyms. I made this decision for several reasons, two in particular.

    First, although I have done my best to create accurate portraits of my research participants, even the most carefully designed narrative cannot capture the complexities of a human life. Nor can it reflect the many nuances of an individual's personal and cultural belief system. Using pseudonyms was a means of acknowledging that even a character in a nonfiction work is a symbol of the individual and not the individual him or herself.

    Second, even before the book came out, I had readers requesting contact information for Amado, Juan Luis, and the other Andeans with whom I worked. This raised serious concerns that once the book was published the individuals whose names appear within it might find themselves besieged with unwanted attention and/or other unforeseen consequences. Such exposure would not only impact the lives of my research participants in a way that they ultimately might not welcome, but could also impact the lives of their families and others around them who had not consented to take part in this study. Preserving their anonymity allowed for our work to be accomplished professionally without unduly impacting their lives.

2. In fact, the word has deeper connotations than that. As Amado explained to me, "The reason I call you Princesa is because in Quechua, the word for *princess* is *ñusta*, which also means Pachamama, or Mother Earth. As a woman, you represent Mother Earth. So, when I say *princess*, I am acknowledging Mother Earth in you."

Chapter Two

1. The efficacy of coca leaf for the relief of altitude sickness is debated. Allen (2002) pointed out that there is little evidence that coca leaf aids in high-altitude adaptation.

2. Barnes (1992) presented the possibility that the tripartite division of the Andean cosmos into three *pachas* may not be aspects of the original Andean metaphysical perspective but rather adopted after the arrival of the Spanish. However, given the

frequency of the "three steps" as a motif included within many Andean antiquities and much of its temple architecture, the consensus among scholars and my research participants is that this is not the case, that the three worlds are indeed an Andean conception.

3. Alternate spellings include *hanan pacha* (Bastien, 1992), *janaj pacha* (Platt, 1997), and *alajjpacha* (Bastien, 1992).

4. An alternate spelling is *aka pacha* (Bastien, 1992).

5. Alternate spellings include *ura pacha* (Bastien, 1992), *uhu* or *uku pacha* (Urton, 1981), and *manqha pacha* (Bastien, 1992).

6. Classen (1993) reported that both the Inca and modern Andeans see the middle section of the body as not only the mediator between top and bottom but also as the center of exchange that controls the flow of fluids through the body. Because of this, Classen stated, in Andean cosmology the middle section of the body is considered the seat of emotion.

7. Several Andean scholars have reflected upon the interrelationship of the human body as microcosm and the cosmos as macrocosm. Classen's (1993) study discussed the ways in which, in Inca cosmology, the human body served both as a symbol and mediator of the cosmic structures and processes.

Classen (1993) wrote,

The fundamental structures of Inca cosmology—the dualities of right and left, high and low, male and female—were, in fact, derived from the structures of the human body. The processes of the body—the intake and outflow of air and fluids, the digestion of food, the circulation of blood, reproduction, aging and death, and so on. (p. 3)

Similarly, Bastien (1978) noted that among the Qollahuayas of Bolivia, the human body functions as a model for ordering society, land, and cosmos. He reports that the Qollahuayas conceptualize the mountain they live on in terms of a body, with the peak as the head, the center as the midsection, and the lower portion as the legs.

Chapter Three

1. Silverblatt (1987) wrote, "The serpent has deep roots in the configuration of Andean symbolic thought. The complex of serpents residing in springs is one manifestation of the Andean concept of the *amaru*. While the *amaru* as symbol encapsulates many referents, one of its principal connotations is that of relation or alliance. This connotation can be extended to the *amaru's* representation of force that erupts when relations of balance and equilibrium are not maintained in the social and natural universe" (p. 192).

Chapter Four

1. Harrison (1989) wrote, "In that white margin of space where Quechua leaves off and English begins, entire worlds shift and revolve, are relinquished or regained" (p. 6).

2. Allen (2002) wrote, "There is an underlying similarity between *tinku* (the encounter) and *ayni* [reciprocal exchange]. Both *tinku* and *ayni* bring equal but opposite parties into relationship with each other; and both may have peaceful or violent manifestations depending on the contexts involved" (p. 178).

3. Some scholars use the word *tinku* in place of *tinkuy*. Allen (2002) explained this distinction by saying, "When streams converge in foaming eddies to produce a single, larger stream they are said to *tinkuy*, and their convergence is called *tinku* (or *tingu*)" (p. 176). However, when asked to explain the difference between the two words, Amado said, "While it is more or less the same thing, there is a difference. *Tinkuy* is more to the point. Anybody can understand *tinkuy*. That's it. But when you say *tinku*, it could be a *tinku* of anything. *Tinku* is like saying 'country,' and *tinkuy* is like saying 'Peru.' *Tinkuy* is more specific."

4. The type and variety of *mesa* objects vary according to region and individual practitioner but most often include (though are not limited to) natural objects (such as stones, feathers, plant and animal materials); religious icons; weaponry (such as swords and daggers); and so on. In the high Andes, *mesas* are usually smaller and simpler than the *mesas* of the north coast, which tend to be bigger and more elaborate. *Mesa* objects are both diagnostic and transformational. Each one is said to hold a particular power or consciousness essential to healing. During the course of a healing, the *mesa* and its objects are "charged" after which, "the accumulated power is 'discharged' or ritually transmitted to the patient" (Joralemon & Sharon, 1993, p. 83).

5. However, this is not always the case. There are reported cases in which shamans represent their *mesas* as a single, indivisible unity. In other cases, one of the three "fields" is significantly bigger than the other two. In others, there are only two fields, the left and the right with no center (Joralemon & Sharon, 1993).

6. This notion of the need for a balancing of the two sides of the *mesa* has been argued against. Claudius Giese argued that "absolute confrontation," not mediation, is the principle against which the *mesa* symbolism is conceived (as cited in Joralemon & Sharon, 1993).

7. The "Master and Slave" analogy also brings up the argument that some have made against the use of "binary classification" as a means by which a culture's ideological structures can be determined. Maybury-Lewis (1989b, p. 112) noted that critics of this form of analysis argue that the presence of hierarchies within these systems negates the balanced symmetry and egalitarianism between the opposites intended by a complementary structure. However, he argued that what seems like an inconsistency is really a reflection of the dialectical nature of balanced dualism. Zuidema (1989) likewise suggested that opposition is not static but that balance involves a movement and countermovement from one side to the other (i.e., outside to the inside, dry season to wet season, male to female, and so on). The balancing occurs over time. As Zuidema said, "Such a temporal point of view helps us to see the roles of [each opposition] not so much in terms of a hierarchical, concentric opposition, but as a diametric, cyclical one" (p. 270). Similarly, Almagor (1989a) asserted, "The trust,

cooperation, and reciprocity engendered through these rituals do not negate the competition, prominence, and achievement that exist in these relationships" (p. 164).

8. Urton (1981) also made mention of the word *cuscan*. This term refers to the union of two equal parts. For instance, in the continuum animate/inanimate, *cuscan* is the point at which an animate unit is in opposition to an equal inanimate unit. Urton emphasized that *cuscan* does not indicate the direction that future changes between the two equal units might take; they are at a state of equilibrium in time and space; subsequent motion may proceed in either (or any) direction.

Chapter Five

1. Creator of time and space.
2. Creator of life.
3. Universal sun.
4. Beginning of life.
5. The one who creates order. The god who brings knowledge and wisdom.
6. Creator of all things.
7. Mother of time and space.
8. In our discussions, Amado and Juan Luis would often use terms from other spiritual or religious traditions such as karma or dharma. Just as anyone with an interest in religious and esoteric themes would, the two of them had picked up much information about other spiritual traditions from books, from television, and from conversations with others about these subjects.
9. When I asked Amado if there was a specific purpose behind the morning beer ritual, he said, "It actually brings you back. It's part of the ceremony. It's don Ignacio's thing, actually. We just kept it because we like it. It's like the festivity part. It's an arrival. A celebration."
10. I asked Amado about the difference between these two words. He said, "*Chaupin* is feminine and *chawpi* is masculine. *Chawpi* is the middle or center of something. Because it is sort of linear and sort of physical, it is male. But *chaupin* is feminine. It's a constant living level of consciousness. It is the infinite equilibrium. It is equilibrium giving birth to equilibrium. While *chawpi* is like the center of the table and that's it." He suggested that in the context of my own experience that I should use the word *chaupin*. I have done so, using *chawpi* only when referring to references made by other scholars.

Chapter 6

1. The etymology of the word *Chavín* is unknown. One suggestion has been that the term comes from the Carib word *chavi* for feline or tiger. Another is that it is a derivation of the Quechua term *chawpin*, meaning "in the center" (Burger, 1995). My Andean participants agreed with this latter translation.
2. Peruvian archaeologist Julio C. Tello believed Chavín to be the "mother culture" of Peruvian civilization. More recently, however, this position has been debated by

scholars such as Kembel (2008), who argued that new research suggests that Chavín de Huántar "was neither the origin site of Andean civilization nor a later center flourishing in the aftermath of the collapse of other monumental centers" (p. 81).

3. The archaeological evidence for the use of the San Pedro cactus during the time of the Chavín civilization is unclear. Burger (1995) reported that San Pedro spines have been uncovered in the ruins of the area's temples, although Torres (2008) stated, "As yet, no remains of visionary plants have been discovered in Chavín archaeological contexts" (p. 239). Most scholars (Burger, 1995; Stone-Miller, 2002; Torres, 2008) point to the frequency of images of the cactus in Chavín's sculpture, carvings, and weavings as evidence that San Pedro played a significant role within the culture.

4. During our conversation, Amado and Juan Luis would use the names *Chavín* and *Chaupin* interchangeably when describing the same geographical location. Chavín is the Spanish version of the area's original name, Chaupin, which, as described in chapter 5, indicates an "intermediate zone" or, as Amado described it, "infinite equilibrium." In order to avoid confusion, I have put "[Chavín]" in places where "Chaupin" was used.

5. *Huachuma* is one of several names applied to the San Pedro cactus.

6. The term *vilca* in Peru is used to refer to a hallucinogenic powder made from the beans of an acacia-like tree (*Anadenanthera colubrine*) (Furst, 1972).

7. Conklin (2008) argued that art is the best means of understanding human minds of the distant past that did not leave written texts, as it carries cultural meaning.

8. Amado said, "The images that we see in the artwork here represent people who received the Medicine's teachings. They are shown with serpents for hair because wisdom is just spilling out."

9. "Yeah . . . three and more!" Amado said when I read him this.

10. Although traditionally scholars such as Rowe (1967) have suggested that the fang motif that reoccurs in Chavín art styles is representative of a feline deity, Burger (1995) pointed out that prominent fangs are also common among other fearsome animals such as the howler monkey, the cayman, the anaconda, and the vampire bat, all of which could have served as inspiration for the Lanzón.

11. So named because of the rectangular projection (tenons) on the back of each stone head. The projections were designed to fit directly into the walls, giving them the appearance of floating in the air without visible support.

REFERENCES

ABC online. (2009, January 20). *World wishes Obama well for inauguration.* Retrieved May 24, 2009, from http://a.abcnews.com/m/screen?id=6685681&pid=76.

Ajaya, S. (1983). *Psychotherapy East and West: A unifying paradigm.* Honesdale, PA: Himalayan Publishers.

Allen, C. J. (2002). *The hold life has: Coca and cultural identity in an Andean community.* Washington, DC: Smithsonian Books. (Original work published 1988)

Almagor, U. (1989a). The dialectic of generation moieties in an East African society. In D. Maybury-Lewis & U. Almagor (Eds.), *The attraction of opposites: Thought and society in the dualistic mode* (pp. 143–169). Ann Arbor: University of Michigan Press.

Almagor, U. (1989b). Dual organization reconsidered. In D. Maybury-Lewis & U. Almagor (Eds.), *The attraction of opposites: Thought and society in the dualistic mode* (pp. 19–32). Ann Arbor: The University of Michigan Press.

Andrien, K. J. (2001). *Andean worlds: Indigenous history, culture and consciousness under Spanish rule 1532–1825.* Albuquerque: University of New Mexico Press.

Ani, M. (1994). *Yurugu: An Afrikan-centered critique of European cultural thought and behavior.* Washington, DC: Nkonimfo.

Apffel-Marglin, F. (1998). Introduction: Knowledge and life revisited. In F. Apffel-Marglin (Ed.), *The spirit of regeneration: Andean cultures confronting western notions of development* (pp. 1–50). London: Zed Books.

Astvaldsson, A. (2000). The dynamics of Aymara duality: Change and continuity in sociopolitical structures in the Bolivian Andes. *Journal of Latin American Studies, 32*(1), 145–174.

Barks, C. (1995). *The essential Rumi.* New York: HarperCollins.

Barnard, A., & Spencer, J. (Eds.). (2002). *Encyclopedia of social and cultural anthropology.* London: Routledge.

Barnes, M. (1992). Catechisms and confessionarios: Distorting mirrors of Andean societies. In R. V. H. Dover, K. E. Seibold, & J. H. McDowell (Eds.), *Andean cosmologies through time: Persistence and emergence* (pp. 67–94). Bloomington: Indiana University Press.

Bastien, J. W. (1978). *Mountain of the condor: Metaphor and ritual in an Andean ayllu.* Prospect Heights, IL: Waveland Press.

Bastien, J. W. (1989). A shamanistic curing ritual of the Bolivian Aymara. *Journal of Latin American Lore, 15*(1), 73–94.

Bastien, J. W. (1992). Shaman versus nurse in an Aymara village: Traditional and modern medicine in conflict. In R. V. H. Dover, K. E. Seibold, & J. H. McDowell (Eds.), *Andean cosmologies through time: Persistence and emergence* (pp. 137–165). Bloomington: Indiana University Press.

Bateson, G. (1991). *A sacred unity: Further steps to an ecology of mind.* San Francisco: Harper Collins.

Bauman, Z. (1993). *Postmodern Ethics.* Cambridge, MA: Blackwell Publishers.

Beattie, J. (1968). Aspects of Nyoro symbolism. *Journal of the International African Institute, 38*(4), 413–442.

Behar, R. (1996). *The vulnerable observer: Anthropology that breaks your heart.* Boston, MA: Beacon Press.

Bischof, H. (2008). Context and contents of early Chavín art. In W. J. Conklin & J. Quilter (Eds.), *Chavín: Art, architecture and culture* (pp. 107–141). Los Angeles: University of California.

Bolin, I. (2006). *Growing up in a culture of respect: Child rearing in highland Peru.* Austin: University of Texas Press.

Box, B., & Frankham, S. (2006). *Cuzco & the Inca heartland* (3rd ed.). Bath, UK: Footprint.

Burger, R. L. (1995). *Chavín and the origins of Andean civilization.* New York: Thames and Hudson.

Caputo, J. D. (1993). *Against ethics: Contributions to a poetics of obligation with constant reference to deconstruction.* Bloomington and Indianapolis: Indiana University Press.

Carpenter, L. K. (1992). Inside/outside. Which side counts?: Duality-of-self and bipartization in Quechua. In R. V. H. Dover, K. E. Seibold, & J. H. McDowell (Eds.), *Andean cosmologies through time: Persistence and emergence* (pp. 115–136). Bloomington: Indiana University Press.

The Center for Nonviolent Communication online. (2005). *Feelings inventory.* Retrieved November 13, 2008, from http://www.cnvc.org/en/learn-online/feelings-list/feelings-inventory.

Chalmers, D. (1995). Facing up to the problem of consciousness. *Journal of Consciousness, Studies 2*(3), 200–219.

Chang, H. (2008). *Autoethnography as method.* Walnut Creek, CA: Left Coast Press.

Classen, C. (1993). *Inca cosmology and the human body.* Salt Lake City: University of Utah Press.

CNN online. (2008, April 21). Peru luxury tourism push met with protest. Retrieved May 5, 2008, from http://www.cnn.com/2008/TRAVEL/getaways/04/21/peru.tourism.ap/index.html.

Conklin, W. J. & Quilter, J. (2008). Introduction. In W. J. Conklin & J. Quilter (Eds.), *Chavín: Art, architecture and culture* (pp. xxvii–xxxii). Los Angeles: University of California.

Cordy-Collins, A. (1977). Chavín art: Its shamanic/hallucinogenic origins. In A. Cordy-Collins & J. Stern (Eds.), *Pre-Columbian art history* (pp. 353–362). Palo Alto, CA: Peek.

Creswell, J. W. (1998). *Qualitative inquiry and research design: Choosing among five traditions*. Thousand Oaks, CA: Sage Publications.

Cruz, A. C. (Speaker). (2007, July 24). *K'intu, waka & pachamama haywa: The fusion of apu, apacheta, ayllu & Altomisayoq within Andean religious practices* (Audio recording). The Heart of the Healer 2007 Gathering, Pisaq, Peru.

Cummins, T. (2008). The felicitous legacy of the Lanzón. In W. J. Conklin & J. Quilter (Eds.), *Chavín: Art, architecture and culture* (pp. 279–304). Los Angeles: University of California.

Dover, R. V. H. (1992). Introduction. In R. V. H. Dover, K. E. Seibold, & J. H. McDowell (Eds.), *Andean cosmologies through time: Persistence and emergence* (pp. 1–16). Bloomington: Indiana University Press.

Edelman, G. M. (1992). *Bright air, brilliant fire: On the matter of the mind*. New York: Basic Books.

Eliade, M. (1959). *Cosmos and history: The myth of the eternal return*. New York: Harper and Row. (Original work published 1954)

Ellis, C. (2004). *The ethnographic I: A methodological novel about autoethnography*. Walnut Creek, CA: AltaMira Press.

Fernandez, E. G. (1998). Development or cultural affirmation in the Andes? In F. Apffel-Marglin (Ed.), *The spirit of regeneration: Andean cultures confronting western notions of development* (pp. 124–139). London: Zed Books.

Fernandez, R. V., & Gutierrez, C. E. (Eds.). (1996). *Andean lives: Gregorio Condori Mamani and Asunta Quispe Huamán*. Austin: University of Texas Press.

Furst, P. T. (1972). *Flesh of the gods: The ritual use of hallucinogens*. Long Grove, IL: Waveland Press.

Glass-Coffin, B. (1991). Discourse, daño and healing in north coastal Peru. *Medical Anthropology, 13*(1–2), 33–55.

Glass-Coffin, B. (1998). *The gift of life: Female spirituality and healing in Northern Peru*. Albuquerque: University of New Mexico Press.

Glass-Coffin, B. (2004). Peruvian shamans. In M. N. Walter & E. J. N. Fridman (Eds.), *Shamanism: An encyclopedia of world beliefs, practices, and culture* (Vol. 1, pp. 439–445). Santa Barbara, CA: ABC-CLIO.

Handwerker, S. E. (2008, August). *The role of consciousness in healing: A humanistic psychotherapeutic approach*. Paper presented at the 2nd Annual Conference of the Society for Humanistic Psychology, Norwood, MA.

Harris, O. (1986). From asymmetry to triangle: Symbolic transformations in northern Potosí. In J. V. Murra, N. Wachtel, & J. Revel (Eds.), *Anthropological history of Andean polities* (pp. 260–280). Cambridge, England: Cambridge University Press.

Harrison, R. (1989). *Signs, songs, and memory in the Andes: Translating Quechua language and culture*. Austin: University of Texas Press.

Harvey, P. (2006). Americas: Native South America (Highland). In A. Barnard & J. Spencer (Eds.), *Encyclopedia of social and cultural anthropology* (pp. 37–40). London: Routledge.

Heckman, A. M. (2003). *Woven stories: Andean textiles and rituals.* Albuquerque: University of New Mexico Press.

Hegel, G. W. F. (1977). *Phenomenology of spirit* (A. V. Miller, Trans.). Oxford, England: Clarendon Press. (Original work published 1804)

Hemingway, E. (1954). *The sun also rises.* New York: Scribner. (Original work published 1926)

Hill, M. D. (2001). *New Age in the Andes: Mystical tourism and cultural politics in Cusco, Peru.* Unpublished doctoral dissertation, Emory University, Atlanta, GA.

Howard-Malverde, R. (1997). Introduction. In R. Howard-Malverde (Ed.), *Creating context in Andean Cultures* (pp. 3–20). Oxford, England: Oxford University Press.

Isbell, B. J. (1978). *To defend ourselves: Ecology and ritual in an Andean village.* Prospect Heights, IL: Waveland Press.

Josephson, B. D., & Rubik, B. A. (1992). The challenge of consciousness research. *Frontier Perspectives, 3*(1), 15–19.

Joralemon, D., & Sharon, D. (1993). *Sorcery and shamanism: Curanderos and clients in northern Peru.* Salt Lake City: University of Utah Press.

Jung, C. G. (1956). *Two essays on analytic psychology* (R. F. C. Hull, Trans.). New York: Meridian Books. (Original work published 1953)

Jung, C. G. (1968). *Psychology and alchemy* (R. F. C. Hull, Trans.). Princeton, NJ: Princeton University Press. (Original work published 1953)

Kehoe, A. B. (2000). *Shamans and religion: An anthropological exploration in critical thinking.* Long Grove, IL: Waveland Press.

Kembel, S. R. (2008). The architecture at the monumental center of Chavín de Huántar: Sequence, transformations, and chronology. In W. J. Conklin & J. Quilter (Eds.), *Chavín: Art, architecture, and culture* (pp. 35–81). Los Angeles: University of California.

Kluger, J. (2007, December 3). What makes us moral? *Time,* 54–60.

Krippner, S. (1992). The shamans as healer and psychotherapist. *Voices, 28*(1), 12–23.

Krippner, S. (2002). Introduction to consciousness studies. In K. McGovern (Ed.), *Learning guide for the nature of consciousness: A survey of contemporary approaches* (pp. 8–13). San Francisco: Saybrook Graduate School and Research Center.

Krippner, S., & Winkler, M. (1995, Summer). Postmodernity and consciousness studies. The Institute of Mind and Behavior, Inc. *The Journal of Mind and Behavior, 16*(3), 255–280.

Lakoff, G., & Johnson, M. (1980). *Metaphors we live by.* Chicago: University of Chicago Press.

León-Portilla, M. (1963). *Aztec thought and culture: A study of the ancient Nahuatl mind* (J. E. Davis, Trans.). Norman: University of Oklahoma Press.

Lévi-Strauss, C. (1963). *Structural anthropology.* New York: Basic Books.

MacCormick, S. (1991). *Religion in the Andes.* Princeton, NJ: Princeton University Press.

Magee, M. (2002). *Peruvian shamanism: The Pachakúti mesa.* Kearney, NE: Middle Field.

#108 10-16-2012 1:12PM
Item(s) checked out to p10758926.

TITLE: Yanantin and Masintin in the Ande
BARCODE: 3 1220 01020 9747
DUE DATE: 11-06-12

Mannheim, B. (1991). *The language of the Inka since the European invasion.* Austin: University of Texas Press.

Maybury-Lewis, D. (1989a). The quest for harmony. In D. Maybury-Lewis & U. Almagor (Eds.), *The attraction of opposites: Thought and society in the dualistic mode* (pp. 1–17). Ann Arbor: University of Michigan Press.

Maybury-Lewis, D. (1989b). Social theory and social practice: Binary systems in central Brazil. In D. Maybury-Lewis & U. Almagor (Eds.), *The attraction of opposites: Thought and society in the dualistic mode* (pp. 97–116). Ann Arbor: University of Michigan Press.

McDowell, J. H. (1992). Exemplary ancestors and pernicious spirits: Sibundoy concepts of culture evolution. In R. V. H. Dover, K. E. Seibold, & J. H. McDowell (Eds.), *Andean cosmologies through time: Persistence and emergence* (pp. 95–114). Bloomington: Indiana University Press.

Murra, J. V., & Wachtel, N. (1986). Introduction. In J. V. Murra, N. Watchel, & J. Revel (Eds.), *Anthropological history of Andean polities* (pp. 1–8). Cambridge, MA: Cambridge University Press.

Needham, R. (Ed.). (1973). *The right and the left: Essays on dual symbolic classification.* Chicago: University of Chicago Press.

Needham, R. (1987). *Counterpoints.* Berkeley and Los Angeles: University of California Press.

Nin, A. (1968). *The novel of the future.* New York: Macmillan Company.

Palomino, S. (1971). Duality in the socio-cultural organization of several Andean populations. *Folk, 13,* 65–88.

Platt, T. (1986). Mirrors and maize: The concept of yanantin among the Macha of Bolivia. In J. V. Murra, N. Wachtel, & J. Revel (Eds.), *Anthropological history of Andean polities* (pp. 228–259). Cambridge, UK: Cambridge University Press.

Platt, T. (1997). The sound of light: Emergent communication through Quechua shamanic dialogue. In R. Howard-Malverde (Ed.), *Creating context in Andean cultures* (pp. 196–226). Oxford, UK: Oxford University Press.

Rabinow, P. (1977). *Reflections on fieldwork in Morocco.* Berkeley and Los Angeles, CA: University of California Press.

Reese, W. L. (1996). *Dictionary of philosophy and religion.* Amherst, NY: Humanity Books.

Richardson, L. (1994). Writing: A method of inquiry. In N. Denzin & Y. Lincoln (Eds.), *Handbook of qualitative research* (pp. 923–948). London: Sage.

Rick, J. W. (2008). Context, construction, and ritual in the development of authority at Chavín de Huántar. In W. J. Conklin & J. Quilter (Eds.), *Chavín: Art, architecture and culture* (pp. 3–34). Los Angeles: University of California.

Rowe, J. H. (1967). Form and meaning in Chavín art. In J. H. Rowe & D. Menzel (Eds.), *Peruvian archeology: Selected readings* (pp. 72–104). Palo Alto, CA: Peek.

Sawada, D., & Caley, M. (1993). Complementarity: A recursive revision appropriate to human science. *Anthropology of Consciousness, 4*(2), 1–8.

Schwarz, M., & Jersey, B. (Producers/Directors). (2008). *Hunting the hidden dimension* [television broadcast]. A Quest Productions and Kikim Media production for NOVA in association with The Catticus Corporation.

Seibold, K. E. (1992). Textiles and cosmology in Choquecancha, Cuzco, Peru. In R. V. H. Dover, K. E. Seibold, & J. H. McDowell (Eds.), *Andean cosmologies through time: Persistence and emergence* (pp. 166–201). Bloomington: Indiana University Press.

Sharon, D. (1972). The San Pedro cactus in Peruvian folk healing. In P. T. Furst (Ed.), *The ritual use of hallucinogens* (pp. 114–135). Long Grove, IL: Waveland Press.

Sherbondy, J. E. (1992). Water ideology in Inca ethnogenesis. In R. V. H. Dover, K. E. Seibold, & J. H. McDowell (Eds.), *Andean cosmologies through time: Persistence and emergence* (pp. 46–66). Bloomington: Indiana University Press.

Silverblatt, I. (1987). *Moon, sun, and witches: Gender ideologies and class in Inca and colonial Peru.* Princeton, NJ: Princeton University Press.

Stone-Miller, R. (2002). *Art of the Andes: From Chavín to Inca.* London: Thames & Hudson.

Sullivan, L. E. (1988). *Icanchu's drum: An orientation to meaning in South American religions.* New York: Macmillan.

Tarnas, R. (1991). *The passion of the Western mind: Understanding the ideas that have shaped our world view.* New York: Ballantine Books.

Taussig, M. (1980). *The devil and commodity fetishism in South America.* Chapel Hill: University of South Carolina Press.

Taylor, E. (in collaboration with S. Krippner). (2000). *Learning guide for Models of Consciousness, course #3040.* San Francisco: Saybrook Graduate School and Research Center.

Torres, C. M. (2008). Chavín's psychoactive pharmacopoeia: The iconographic evidence. In W. J. Conklin & J. Quilter (Eds.), *Chavín: Art, architecture and culture* (pp. 239–259). Los Angeles: University of California.

Urton, G. (1981). *At the crossroads of earth and sky: An Andean cosmology.* Austin: University of Texas Press.

Urton, G. (1999). *Inca myths.* London: British Museum Press.

Vasquez, G. R. (1998). The ayllu. In F. Apffel-Marglin (Ed.), *The spirit of regeneration: Andean cultures confronting western notions of development* (pp. 89–123). London: Zed Books.

Watts, A. (1969). *The two hands of God: The myths of polarity.* Toronto: Collier Books.

Webb, H. S. (2007). *Pilot study: An autoethnographic exploration of Andean complementary dualism.* Unpublished manuscript, Saybrook University, San Francisco, CA.

Wilcox, J. P. (1999). *Keepers of the ancient knowledge: The mystical world of the Q'ero Indians of Peru.* Boston, MA: Element.

Williams, M. (2005). *Problems of knowledge: A critical introduction to epistemology.* Oxford, UK: Oxford University Press.

Zuidema, R. T. (1989). The moieties of Cuzco. In D. Maybury-Lewis & U. Almagor (Eds.), *The attraction of opposites: Thought and society in the dualistic mode* (pp. 255–275). Ann Arbor: University of Michigan Press.

Zuidema, R. T. (1992). Inca cosmos in Andean context: From the perspective of the Capac Raymi Camay Quilla feast celebrating the December solstice in Cuzco. In R. V. H. Dover, K. E. Seibold, & J. H. McDowell (Eds.), *Andean cosmologies through time: Persistence and emergence* (pp. 17–45). Bloomington: Indiana University Press.

INDEX

Page numbers in italic text indicate illustrations.

absolutism, 185*n7*
Akashic Records of Mother Earth, 153
alchemy, 82
Allen, C. J., 41, 45, 66, 75, 140
altitude sickness. See *sorache*
Amado, 19, 110, 162, 187*n1*; on adaptability, 57; on Andean cosmos, 44–45; on *ayni*, 41; background of, 24; on Chavín, 92; on death, 111–12; on energy blockages, 44; on *hanaq pacha*, 41; as healer and teacher, 25; Juan Luis compared to, 35–36; on *kay pacha*, 42; on Lanzón, 96, 102; on nothingness, 31; on *pachacuti*, 51; on reaction to energy, 107–8; on reality, 29, 175; on unpartnered people, 139
Andean cosmos: Amado on, 44–45; Christianity incompatibility with, 44–45; on destiny, 108; energies of, 41, 187*n2*; on good and evil, 106, 108, 113–14, 176; on karma, 112; on murder, 108, 109; reincarnation and, 112–13

Andean epistemological system: integration of, 28; relationship between entities and energy in, 30
Andean ideology: on creation, 54; Fernandez on, 6; inclusiveness of, 5; on time and space, 51–52
Andean model: of reality, 30, 65, 70, 72; of time and space, 53
Andean people, *136*, 183*n1*, 183*n3*; marriage of, 4, 140; world as dialectical process for, 64–65
Andean philosophy: complementary dualism allegiance of, 4, 6; Glass-Coffin on, 73–74; global interaction and, 178; ideological commitment within, 23; illness and, 43; on male and female polarity, 137, 140; mind or spirit or soul perceived by, 40; symbols and, 120; Taoism compared to, 2; understanding of, 16; Western culture compared to, 120, 175–78
Andean shaman, 43, 67
Ani, M., 52–53
animals, 94–95, 191*n8*. *See also* condor; puma; serpent
antagonistic split, in Western philosophical models, 2